—I Walk by— Faith, Not by — Sight —

Beatrice Guzzi

ISBN 978-1-64349-977-2 (paperback)
ISBN 978-1-64349-978-9 (digital)

Christian Faith Publishing, Inc.
832 Park Avenue
Meadville, PA 16335
www.christianfaithpublishing.com

Printed in the United States of America

To God, my husband, and my family
who've made my life worth it all.

Part 1

"You will be blind within three to twenty years."

These are the words that had been spoken to me by my eye doctor. Early that spring, I felt I needed to have my eyes examined as I was having trouble reading my cookbooks. I was a young bride of only one year at the time, and I always had problems with my sight. I just thought I needed a new prescription for my lenses.

My husband, Jim, and I went to see his eye doctor in Jersey City, New Jersey. His name was Doctor Brophy. He examined me and told me that I was considered legally blind—meaning, I could see but could not drive. He decided to refer me to his brother, who was a surgeon, to get another opinion. The following week, I went to see him, and he ran many more tests. I was told to come back the next week again. Well, the next week came. I was there and never thought I would ever hear these words.

He said, "It kills me to say this to you, Bea, but you have RP—retinitis pigmentosa. It is a deterioration of the retina, and unfortunately, it causes blindness. You will be blind within three to twenty years." To say I was shocked was an understatement. Nothing could be done. No surgery. No cure. Nothing! I always knew I had poor vision. I also knew that if something was bad, wouldn't it get worse? Of course, but I never wanted to think of this. Well, I was numb after hearing this horrible news. And I knew which way I was heading—into darkness.

Nothing Jim and I said to each other would help. It was just, "I can't believe it." We drove back to my parent's house in Hoboken where Jim and I were raised. We grew up together on the same block. At the age of sixteen, we started to go out together. Even though we knew each other all our lives, we never got along as kids. He was such a tease! One day, when he made me cry, my grandmother told him she would sit on him and make a pancake out of him as she was over two hundred pounds. But I got him back by marrying him because now he was going to be stuck with a blind wife. That would really flatten anyone out!

When we walked in the door and told my parents and grandmother the news, they could not believe it. They were in awe. They immediately called my uncle, Carl, who was the top surgeon at the time at Saint Mary's Hospital in Hoboken, New Jersey. He referred me to a specialist in New York City, which gave me some hope. His name was Doctor Cole. It was like in the movies, when the girl goes to a great doctor and he has all the answers. Well, no such luck. After seeing him and all the examinations he put me through, I still couldn't see anything. Afterward, he said to me very coldly, "Yes, you have RP. Next patient, please."

I asked if anything could be done. He said, "No."

When we got home to my parent's house and told them the outcome, they started to blame each other as RP is hereditary. For the first time in her life, my grandmother was at a loss for words. She was the one I always counted on to bring me out of a bad situation or to give me some words of encouragement. But today, nothing was said. She just looked at me with the most forlorn expression. I laid across her bed and cried my heart out.

I had such a great relationship with my grandmother. She was like a second mother to me. Whenever I was hurt by someone or something, she was there for me and would listen to my sob stories. She would hold me in her big arms, listen to me, and give me some wise advice. Then she would say, "Come on, let's go have some tea and Social Tea cookies." My grandmother and I were very close. However, she was a very tough woman. She liked to control the household as it was her house we all lived in together, and my father wasn't too happy about that. This was very upsetting to me as I loved them both. Living in a volatile Italian family, there are a lot of arguments, but you get used to it. The one thing that was always there was a lot of love and security.

I was very sensitive as a girl. I remember walking home from school after a hard day or after being hurt by someone saying something mean. When I saw St. Ann's Roman Catholic Church we lived next to, and my house came into view, my whole body would relax. I knew I was almost home into the love and safety of my family. We lived in a seven-room apartment on the first floor of a five-family building owned by my grandfather. I was the youngest of three children. Rae, Carl, and I were third-generation Italian-Americans.

Paternal grandparents Robert and Raffaela Cricco

My grandfather came here to the United States at the age of five, but my grandmother was born here in Newark, New Jersey. They owned a metal novelty company and worked very hard in their factory. My grandmother told me how she had to sew doll clothing at home to earn money for four years so that my grandfather could get his business up and running. My grandfather became very successful and had two hundred people working for him. He was so generous to us and many people, and was very loved by all who knew him. When he died at the young age of fifty-nine, it was a tragedy to us all.

Parents Joseph and Frances Cricco

My dad loved and admired his father so much. He was distraught and couldn't handle the loss. After a few years, we lost the business as a result. It was a very rough time for my parents and their marriage, but with the help of God, and my wonderful mother who stuck by him through it all, he got back on track. My dad started his own painting business. Before long, he had forty men working for him with four trucks for the equipment. My dad was a very proud man, and even though his friends deserted him, he pulled himself up and did what he had to do so that he could gain his self-respect and love from his family.

In my eyes as a child, my daddy could do anything, fix everything, and could make it all better. I remember one of my young cousins on my mother's side of the family, who was only four years old, had broken a glass. His mother was so upset, but he said, "Don't worry, Mommy, Uncle Joe can fix it." And I wanted a husband that could fix anything and show me unconditional love like my dad did when I was a kid.

Jim and I were sixteen years old when we met. We hung out together with our friends in a group, and I really didn't think anything of him at the time. I was actually seeing one of Jim's best friends, but my girlfriend brought out Jim's good qualities that I wasn't aware of; and soon after, we started dating. My other girlfriend wasn't too happy as she really liked Jim, but I knew he didn't feel the same about her, and I knew his mother already had her eye on me.

We lived down the street from each other, and our families knew each other quite well. Our grandmothers were best friends. Although his grandmother died before ever knowing about us dating, my family was all in favor of us going steady. But it wasn't until after seeing the movie *A Summer Place* with Sandra Dee and Troy Donahue that I knew he was the one. That movie really made us fall in love; and ultimately, the soundtrack "Theme from a Summer Place" went on to be our wedding song. I always prayed to God to send me the right person, and He did.

Jim was everything I wanted in a boyfriend. He was kind, considerate, and had a good personality. It also helped that he was good looking. He could carry on a conversation with anyone when he was young, and I liked that because at that age, a lot of boys were very shy, and you literally had to pull the words out of them. I had dated a lot before Jim at that young age; however, Jim did not. He flirted a lot, but he didn't have anyone special before me. Even though he was a great guy, he had his faults too. He was spoiled, very controlling, and we fought a lot. We still do, but I refused to have someone tell me what to do. I always stood up to him and anyone else. I guess that is why we have lasted so long. I don't think he would have wanted a pushover. I refuse to be a "Yes, dear" wife!

Bea and Jim's Wedding April 18th 1964

On April 18, 1964, we were married. It was a beautiful day. My sister was my maid of honor, and my sister-in-law, Joyce, and Jim's cousin, Rita, were my bridesmaids. My brother was Jim's best man, and his friends Joe and Anthony were his groomsmen. I wore a lovely lace wedding ball gown. It had long sleeves with a sweetheart neckline. I wore a crystal crown on my head with a veil attached. I felt like a princess, and that day I was going to be married to my prince. I couldn't believe this day had finally come.

Jim was waiting for me at the altar as I walked down the aisle with my dad on my arm. I felt like the luckiest girl in the world. I remember wanting to take flowers to the Blessed Mother, but I was nervous that I would trip on my big gown. Jim took my hand, and said to me, "I'll take you, honey." Little did I know he would be taking me by the hand for the rest of my life. We didn't have a fancy catering hall, just a nice hall for small weddings. Our parents didn't have a lot of money, so they did what they could, and God bless my grandmother for paying for my gown. We honeymooned at Honeymoon Haven in the Pocono Mountains in Pennsylvania. It rained all week, but do you think we cared? We then went to live down the shore at my father-in-law's summerhouse, which didn't last too long.

Maternal grandparents Frank and Faustina Rondinone

I think we both thought our families had a lot of money, but we were wrong. Outside appearances looked like our families were doing very well. The truth be told, they were just making it. But one thing we both had in common was a lot of love and respect for our parents, despite their faults. They worked very hard to raise us, with the help of God, and their good works resulted in raising good kids. This was the most important factor in both of our lives. Our moms brought us up in the Catholic faith at Saint Ann's Church that just happened to be on the corner of our street. There were no excuses not to go, and our lives centered around church. We went to mass every Sunday, went to Sunday school, played in the churchyard, and went roller skating in the church hall where different affairs were held. And coincidentally, that's where I broke my arm, and my mom hid my skates after that. We also went on Confraternity of Christian Doctrine trips. I remember going to New York, and going to an indoor pool. This was my first experience in an indoor pool, and I didn't like it. I was so used to going to Erskine Lakes in Ringwood, New Jersey. There was a lake community where my grandparents had a summer home, and I'd spend all of my summers there for the next twenty years. I knew I was very blessed as a young girl, especially when I got to go swimming in the lake, and I thought about my poor friends who were stuck in the hot city. I felt so sorry for them.

First Holy Communion

Yes, God was a great part of my life. I loved going to church when I was a little girl. I would stop in and say a few prayers before going home to eat lunch as my school was only across the street. I remember the peaceful silence of the church, and I loved being alone in there. Just me and God. I'm so glad I spent a lot of time in Saint Ann's as it is really a beautiful church. I saw it so much that I can still tell you where everything is. It had a high dome ceiling with marble pillars and ornate gold light fixtures. My grandmother always sat next to the second pillar. All the pews were carved on the outside, and had a dark wooden finish. The altar was made of white marble, and it was very high. In the middle of the top of the altar was a niche with a statue of Saint Ann and her precious daughter, the Blessed Mother. Below was the altar table that held the tabernacle where the Blessed Sacrament was enclosed. It had a beautiful gold case with a cross on top, and a little gold mesh curtain in front. It also held two candelabras where five candles were lit, and a large Bible on a stand.

On the right side of the main altar was another altar that held Saint Anthony holding infant Jesus, and a candleholder made of black wrought iron. Behind him, the top of the wall was painted in blue, and the bottom half was marble. On the left side of the main altar was another altar holding the Blessed Mother and more candles. It only cost ten cents to have a candle lit for a special intention to Our Lady.

Along the side walls were beautiful stained-glass windows. Between the windows were niches holding other life-sized statues of saints with shelves holding large candles, and on the side of them were pictures of the stations of the cross. They depicted Jesus' birth, life, and suffering until his death on the cross. The walls were a cream color on top, and the bottom was lined with marble in different shades of tan, brown, and gold. In the back of the church there were the confessionals. Along the back in the left corner was a little chapel with the Blessed Mother holding Jesus on her lap after he suffered and died on the cross. There was a tiny stained-glass window, and it also had candles to light. Every time I went in there, I was overcome with such a profound sense of sadness.

The entrance to the church had three doors—the main entrance, and two side doors that had a very large cross holding our Lord Jesus. And on the far right was a small room that held the baptismal font. On the left was a door going up to the choir loft that was over the rear of the church. In front of the choir loft was a big clock. I guess this was so the priest could see the time and not take too long with his homily. In the entry of the church, on each side of the main doors, stood two white marble angels holding holy water. The floors were made of marble as well. It was awesome. I would stand in the rear of the church and look down the aisle. My eyes drank in every part of that magnificent place that held the spirit of my Lord and Savior. I'm so glad I memorized every inch of this beautiful church as a little girl. Little did I know I'd never get to see it again or until, hopefully, God restored my sight.

First Holy Communion

I know now, after so many years, a lot has changed, but it is kept beautifully maintained by the parishioners. The outside of the church has large stone steps leading up to the three sets of double doors. The church is made of tan bricks that extend up to a point. On the roof is a high steeple that houses the most beautiful sounding bells that have ever been heard. The rectory is attached to the church that makes it easy for the priests to enter and conduct mass. In front of the churchyard is a statue of Our Lady of Fatima. On the side of the pedestal is inscribed, "Donated by Mr. and Mrs. Robert P. Cricco," my grandparents. We could look out of our kitchen window and see it. Now they have placed the statue closer to the rectory, and placed a statue of Saint Ann in its place, which was more logical as this is the saint the church is named after. I thank God for this church and all its memories—especially walking down that long aisle to Jim on my wedding day. Whenever we visit, I feel like I'm home!

While growing up, you were told if you weren't good, God would punish you. That was before I learned we had a loving God, not someone who was out to get you. My faith was also formed by my grandma who told me stories about the saints. At that time as Catholics, we never read the Bible, only the missal. We said our rosary, went to mass every Sunday and holy day, and went to confession every Saturday or you couldn't receive communion. Like the Jews, we had a lot of rules and regulations. For instance, you couldn't eat meat on Fridays, couldn't eat before receiving communion, and couldn't do anything of amusement on Good Friday. I loved my faith, and did what I was asked to do. This was all before Vatican II when all the rules were changed.

Confirmation   Confirmation with sister
                                Rae and brother Carl

At the age of twelve, after I received my confirmation, I did not want to go to Sunday school anymore. I remember getting out of line after mass, running home, and Father Joe running after me. As soon as my grandma spoke to him, I was excused from going. Now I wasn't spoiled, but I did get my way most of the time as the youngest of three children. Being the baby of the family comes with many perks.

I really didn't come to the Lord until many years later. I became a born-again Christian, which means asking Jesus into your heart, making him first in your life, and putting him in complete control. When you do this, you have complete trust and faith in God. By reading the Bible, I learned precisely what God did for me. He gave us his only precious son to save us from our sins. My Jesus is the light of my life. All mankind can come to Him, and He will welcome anyone with open arms. It is so simple. You ask Him to come into your heart, and make Him Lord and master of your life. You must repent of your sins, and the Holy Spirit will come into you as it did with me, and will reside there forever. You must also tell someone that you have accepted Jesus Christ into your heart. This confession of faith must be stated by you to affirm your true feelings. It is so wonderful and comforting to know that you are not walking through this life alone. You have a true friend walking beside you forever, and that is such a fantastic feeling. I don't know how I could have gotten through all I have without my faith in Jesus. When I start talking about my Lord, I can go on forever.

Now, to get back to the worst time of my life. After Jim and I went home to our apartment, I was in such a depressed state. I felt like my whole life would take a big change. Could I handle it? Well, did I have a choice? I moved around my apartment like a robot, not knowing what to do first, so I didn't do anything but sulk. There was such a heavy feeling on my chest and in my heart that I couldn't get rid of. I guess I had all of the feelings someone has when they have lost a loved one through death, and that was exactly the way I felt. I had all the same raw emotions. I was angry and hurt that God could let this happen to me when I did all the right things to be a good person. I was depressed. I felt hopeless. In my anger, one day, I told Jim to go back to his dad and leave me alone as I didn't want him to be stuck with a blind wife. He said the words I will never forget. "We got married for better or for worse, in sickness and in health, 'til death do us part." He added, "If it were me, would you leave?"

I said, "I would never." And later on, I had a chance to prove that to him. But I know now that I had to work at being a total woman like he deserved.

One day, I was watching television, which I did a lot at the time. After all, what else was I to do except feel sorry for myself? I'll never forget what was on: the soap opera, General Hospital. The actor was playing a recovering alcoholic, and I heard the Serenity Prayer. "God, grant me the serenity to accept the things I cannot change, courage to change the things I can, and wisdom to know the difference." That prayer changed my life. I knew I couldn't change the fact that I was going blind, but I could change my attitude, which I did immediately.

I got up from the sofa, walked over to my kitchen phone, and called The Commission of the Blind. My doctor had given me the number, but earlier, I couldn't bring myself to call. That would be like me admitting the truth, and I was not ready to do that. But now I knew I had to come to terms with my future and deal with it. A week later, they sent a counselor to explain what they do, and what they'd do to try and help me learn how to live in a world without sight. They also sent a homemaker to teach me how to perform housework and cooking without seeing. She really didn't have to explain too much as I had already been using my other senses to help perform these tasks without even realizing I was. The instructor taught me how to read and write braille with a slate and stiles as I wanted to be able to read cookbooks due to my love of cooking. I was given very large books that I studied and practiced reading.

Reading braille

Learning to read braille is very difficult, but I accomplished it in only two months. It was like learning a different language, but I was determined. I would wake up every morning, clean my house, and start teaching myself. I worked at it all day until almost five o'clock in the evening when I would start dinner. After I learned how to read Grade 1 braille, I had to learn Grade 2 braille—which was even harder as it focused on contractions—but I did it.

After I mastered braille, they sent me a mobility instructor. She showed me how to get around with a walking cane. This was difficult for me as I had to go outside into the big bad world. I asked myself many times if I was going to be able to do this, but I had to. This was my life now, and I had to do it or stay forever housebound. At the age of twenty-three, I wasn't about to let that happen to me. It was easy to walk outdoors when I had my instructor right behind me, but when she'd call and tell me I was on my own, I was petrified.

Reading a braille recipe book

I prayed a lot, but the driving force was the good Lord helping me and reminding me that I could do this. I had such a yearning to have children, so I felt I must succeed—especially if they were going to have a mother who was blind, but someone they could depend on no matter what. I asked, "What if they needed me to go to the store, and get milk for them?" I would have to do it, and I forced myself to get out there.

Another driving force for me was when Jim was drafted into the army. The Vietnam War was going on. He was accepted and was expected to go. Okay, now what would I do? I'd have to go back home to live with my parents, and I certainly did not want to do that! I prayed, of course, and Jim and I did something about it. We went to our church and asked Father Sal, the priest who performed our marriage ceremony, to write a letter to the Secretary of Defense to see if Jim could be excused. We asked my father-in-law to help as well since he knew some people in high places. My father knew some influential people too, but a lot of his friends were no longer around as they abandoned him when he lost my grandfather's business. I was really hurt by him as he always bragged about knowing everyone who was a "someone." In a way, I felt sorry for him, but I needed help from whomever I could get it from.

Jim wanted to help his country, but he had his own turmoil at home and didn't want to leave at this tragic time in my life. Well, God came through for us, although it was not the way I wanted to hear it. Jim was excused from service due to a hardship case. I was very upset to hear that I was a hardship to him. I said, "I never wanted to be a hardship to anyone, especially to you." This gave me more persistence to be as independent as I could possibly be.

At the time, Jim was working three jobs to keep on top of our bills, and I was of no help to him in this area. He was working for the Elastic Stop Nut Company. This was a government job where he assembled nuts and bolts in their factory. He despised doing this, but it put food on the table and paid the bills. He worked three nights a week at a Shell gas station in town, and also for his father's limousine service on the weekends. Jim was a mechanic by trade and vowed to own his own service station someday; but until then, he had to do what he had to do.

One night we had a very bad argument. Jim said the words I will never forget as long as I live. We women have a long, long memory! He said the words I thought I would never hear him say. "You are nothing but a hardship to me." I was mortified. When he saw the look on my face, he knew he hurt me very badly. He took me in his arms, and tried to apologize, but I have never forgotten it. That was another reason why I had to be as independent as I could be. If he grew tired of me, I would have to do it on my own. I made it my business to learn everything I possibly could, to take care of myself, if my life were to go in that direction.

My sister, Rae, played a big part in helping me overcome my fear. God bless her. She gave me a lot of pep talks to build up my courage. The first time I ventured out, I walked across the street to the card store. Before I left, I prayed and carried my rosary beads in my pocket. I started crossing the side street first. I lived on the corner of Passaic Avenue and Main Street, in the very heart of Chatham, New Jersey. Luckily for me, there was a traffic light on the corner, and sometimes a policeman was present. As I became more comfortable, I went out quite often. I'd walk over to my sister's house about a block and a half away. To get there, I had to cross Main Street—which is actually Route 24—and a main highway. Was I scared? You bet I was. But I did it until one day, I was almost killed.

I stood at the corner as usual, and listened for the traffic to stop in front of me. I heard the motors starting to move on the side street, so I proceeded to go ahead. A big truck was running the red light, and only by the grace of God was I saved. I felt a big hand on my arm as I was pulled back. Thank God, the policeman was there! After thanking him, he went over to the truck and gave the man a ticket. I continued to walk over to my sister's house and when I arrived, I told her what happened. She didn't get upset and proceeded to instruct me as I was babysitting for her that day. I could not believe how she could be so unfeeling. Many years later, I commented on it and how she made me feel. She said, "I had to be tough." She was right, but it really hurt me. I must admit my sister did give me a lot of support and pushed me very hard. It's because of her encouragement, the love of my husband, and my faith in God that today I am as tough as I am. I have to be!

Let me tell you more about my sister Rae. She was seven years old, and my brother Carl was four years old when I was born. Since they were three years apart, they got along better and had more in common with each other. My sister has a great personality. She's smart, and God gave her a wonderful gift enabling her to play the piano very well. What my sister lacks in height, being only five feet tall, she makes up in her friendly manner. She has a way of drawing you in and immediately liking her.

As a child, I truly admired her, but was a little intimidated. She liked to argue and loved debating. She was always adamant about proving a point. Being as smart as she was, she always thought she was right. I was the complete opposite. I hated confrontations; but if I felt I was right, I would argue my point. Let's face it, doesn't everyone feel that way? I guess I took after my mother who always wanted peace and minimal conflict. When Rae and I disagree on something, I let her have her way, accept her the way she is, and love her anyway. I'll always be very proud of her.

I remember when she graduated from high school. She had to play the piano at her graduation. My grandmother sewed very well and made her a beautiful green velvet dress with fur on the hem of the neckline. To me, she looked absolutely beautiful. She didn't think she was very good looking, and she thought she was a little chubby; but that night, she looked like an angel. She played "Malaguena" perfectly. I was so proud of her, I thought my heart would burst. After high school, she went to secretarial school and landed a job in New York. One day, she invited me to lunch and to see her office. It was so exciting for me being in the big city, and I remember we had Chinese food.

Sister Rae and her husband Peter Harff

My sister married a great guy named Peter Harff. She met him at the lake where we spent our summers as he was a lifeguard. One day, he gave her a pin to keep her bathing suit up as her strap had broken. I guess you can say they were pinned together for life. After living in Jersey City for a while, they moved to Chatham. Pete needed to live along the train line since he worked in Harrison at RCA Electronics as a mechanical engineer. They had three beautiful children, Paula, David, and Michael. I always babysat them, and I just loved Chatham. When I first saw this beautiful town, I thought it was right out of a story book. It was nothing like the city I was used to. I hoped and prayed that one day, when I was married, I could live there as well. Fortunately for me, that day came true.

My sister and I became much closer after I was married, and we had much more in common. Rae taught me how to cook and bake. Although I learned at home, by watching my mom, I was given very little opportunity to gain hands-on experience. My mom, dad, and grandmother were always at the stove, and I didn't get to cook very often. They always had to put their own "special" ingredients into everything they made, so I never felt as though it was done by myself. If it wasn't for Rae teaching me, and watching my mom, I wouldn't be the great cook and baker I am today.

Many years later, Rae and her family moved to Long Island, New York. RCA was taken over by General Electric, and Pete had received a new job position. It was hard to see them leave, but the move changed their lives. For in Long Island is where she and her family found the Lord, and in such a profound way.

Pete was Protestant, and we were Catholics. It was not easy for them to marry at that time, but they were allowed if he promised to raise the children Catholic. They did not worship together, but this was something my sister always prayed they would do. Well, she had her prayers answered when she decided to attend a non-denominational church. She was going to a prayer group, and the people were so insistent that she go to their church as she was not too happy at the Catholic church she was currently attending. It was very large, and she didn't feel any warmth there. Rae was used to a small church, and although it was quite different than the Catholic church, she felt the warmth and love right away. She and her family gave their lives to Jesus. It was the most wonderful feeling to be able to worship with her husband, and pray together with her family. Rae who is very outgoing, along with her family, became very involved in the church. So much so that many years later her son, David, even became a children's pastor.

When Pete was sixty-one years old, he died of cancer. This was very hard for my sister and her family. Living so far away from her made it difficult to help, but her church family did. A year later, she moved to Pennsylvania to be near her daughter, son, and their families. She is very happy living there, and is very involved in her new church. Rae has a very nice gentleman companion named Bob. He taught her how to golf, and they're going on a lot of cruises together. They live in the same town, but they don't want to get married or live together. Things are great the way they are.

My sister worked many years as a secretary for her church, and it is so wonderful to see her enjoying herself now. She really deserves it, and I am so happy for her. Her daughter, Paula, has three sons, and she is a nurse conducting research for cystic fibrosis. Her husband, David, is a great guy. Rae's youngest son, Michael, and his wife, Monica, live close by with their son. Rae's son, David, and his wife, Kristine, along with their four children, still live in Long Island near his church.

If I lost my sight when I was living at home, my mom wouldn't have let me do a thing. But I was blessed to be living near my sister when I went blind as siblings are a little tougher, and they don't have the same fears a mother has. Rae and the good Lord helped me pull up my inner strength, and therefore I was able to believe in myself. This also gave me the self-esteem I needed to see that I had the capability to do anything I wanted in my life. Thank God!

My brother, Carl, was the prince of our house. That's how it is in an Italian family. The way I saw it, the sun rose on my sister and set on my brother. And for me, I was the baby of the family and usually got whatever I wanted. If I didn't, I would cry and go to my grandmother with whom we lived. She would inevitably give me what I wanted. Now I wasn't spoiled, I just had a way of getting what I wanted by crying or going to my grandma.

Carl was four years older than me, and he loved to tease me. He loved to see me cry, which I did very often. I was so sensitive that if anyone said or did anything to me, I would cry. Then my father would sing the words, "Without a tear, the day would never end," and I would cry even more! My brother was small, but he was tough, and he wasn't afraid of anyone. My dad was also good at boxing and taught Carl how to fight—not necessarily to start fights, but to defend himself. We weren't very close growing up as he went into high school when I was in grade school, and we didn't have much in common. He didn't graduate high school, but went into the army, and got his GED. Before he enlisted, he tried to keep a watch on me as I was feeling full of myself at the age of fourteen. I turned out to be pretty good looking, and at that age you felt like you were something else.

When I went out, he would follow me thinking I was going out with a boy, and I was mortified. I felt it wasn't his place or up to him to tell me what to do. I felt it was up to my father to tell him; but at the time, my father wasn't home that often as he was going through his own personal hell. I think Carl saw my mother was always nervous about letting me out alone, so he watched out for me. I thought this wasn't right for an older brother to do as he wasn't my father, and there was a lot of resentment. Needless to say, I was really happy when he went off to the army. But as time went on, I grew up, and I understood why he did what he felt he had to do to protect me. After he returned home, he and I got along much better. I suppose it was due to the fact that I had grown up and started going out with Jim. Carl liked Jim as he knew his family for most of his life, which made it much easier for us to date.

Not long after his return, Carl met a wonderful girl, and her name was Joyce. He met her at a dance at the lake where she was visiting a friend. Joyce had just graduated from nursing school when they met. They dated for a couple of years, and soon after they were married. They moved to the lake where they stayed at my parent's summer home, and later bought a house nearby. Carl and Joyce went on to have six children. They had a little girl who was born with many defects, and unfortunately, she died after only five months. Her name was Denice. Shortly after, they had two sons, Joseph and Carl, then three girls, Christine, Cara, and Caryn.

Brother Carl Cricco and his wife Joyce

Many years later, they decided to move to Cape Cod, Massachusetts. My brother and his wife had honeymooned there, and they fell in love with the area. At the time, Carl was working with Dad in his painting business, and handled all the paper hanging, which he was very good at. Joyce was a nurse and could get a job in any hospital. They bought a property with a house and eight cottages that the kids helped maintain. They rented the cottages out during the summer. As time went on, the kids grew and married and they sold the cottages. Sadly, Carl didn't take care of himself. He drank, smoked, and ate too much. He had high blood pressure, and bad kidneys, and had to go on dialysis treatment. He died at the age of seventy. Joyce was then diagnosed with uterine cancer and passed away a few years later.

When they lived in Jersey, we got together very often. However, after they moved, we only saw each other every once in a long while. Going to Cape Cod was a six-hour drive, and too far for just a weekend visit. But when we did go, we had a great time. My brother was a lot of fun to be with. We'd get together, all his eleven grandchildren would come along, there was always a lot of laughs, and of course a lot of food. Carl loved to cook and eat, just like any other Italian. I really miss all the times he would call and ask me for a recipe. Usually, it was one of my mom's that he had forgotten. Yes, I do miss him, and I wish I could be there more with my nieces and nephews. I try to call, but with them working and taking care of their children, it's hard to find the right time to talk. They're great kids, and I do love them very much.

Part 2

Jim and I really wanted to have children, but for some reason it was very difficult for us. I guess it wasn't God's will. I prayed a lot, but nothing was happening. At this time, we were married for about three years. We went for many tests, and nothing was wrong. I kept asking myself, "What was the matter with me?" Well, there wasn't anything wrong, it just wasn't the right time. I started to feel as though I wasn't meant to have any children, and I contemplated going to work to teach braille for the Commission of the Blind.

The year 1967 had to be the worst year of my life as this was when I lost my sight—exactly three years from when the doctor told me I would. I was hoping it wouldn't happen. Then I lost my grandmother, and I had a miscarriage. Talk about horror stories! My vision was rapidly failing, so I took out my contact lenses as they were of no use any longer. I remember going to bed one night, and looking toward my windows, and I couldn't see my red and white drapes. I started to cry and told Jim. He took me in his arms and told me it would be okay. He said, "We'll get through this together."

The next day, I walked over to my sister's house. I went to her bathroom and when I looked into the mirror, I couldn't see myself. For a long time, I would get at least a small glimpse of my face as she had a bright light over the mirror. But this time, I could not. I came out and told my sister, and she just hugged me. After all, what could she say? As time went on, I had a little bit of peripheral vision on each side of my eyes, although it was quite distorted. For instance, a straight pole would look like a squiggly line. People's faces were distorted and very hard to make out. This was the beginning of the end—although for many years, I could get a glimpse of light if I was passing by a lamp. Then after a while, nothing.

For me to know if a light is on, I must feel the bulb for heat or feel for the switch to be up for on, or down for off. The only good thing is I don't need the lights on. To try and describe what my eyes see, it's all gray. Not blackness; just a fog of black and white speckles, and thin lines going in all directions. If you've had a black and white television going out of focus, you can understand what I'm describing. It would get snowy with lines going in different directions. But I don't concentrate on what my eyes see. I picture where I am or what I'm doing. I'm very thankful that I was able to see beforehand, for if someone describes scenery to me, I'm able to imagine it and picture it in my mind.

March seventh of that year, my grandmother died. She had been hospitalized prior with a failing heart, and had to have her leg removed due to diabetes that came on later in life. I was devastated. Not only did I lose my grandmother, but I lost my best friend and confidant all rolled into one. I couldn't get beyond it. I missed her so much that one day I called her phone number. I just wanted to hear her voice again. It just rang and rang.

Soon after, I found out I was pregnant. I was so excited! But six weeks later, I was rushed to the hospital and I had a miscarriage. The next day, my doctor called and told me that they could not hear a heartbeat. I was heartbroken. My mom tried to console me by saying, "It was probably for the best as the baby might have been sick or deformed." Somehow that didn't help me much. I remember it was Halloween, and children were coming to the door for trick or treat, which made it even worse. That night, Jim and I got together with our neighbors and had a few drinks. I drank too much as I was trying to get rid of the pain. The next day, I had such a headache that when the phone rang, it sounded like Big Ben. It was a stupid thing to do as I knew I couldn't wash away pain by drinking.

My dad taught me a big lesson about overdrinking. When I was sixteen, at Thanksgiving dinner, I was very thirsty after eating too much. He gave me a glass of sparkling wine, and I really liked it. He said, "Here have some more." He kept on pouring me wine.

After drinking four glasses, I got up and felt very dizzy and sick to my stomach. He said, "Don't forget how you feel now, and maybe you will think twice before getting drunk." That was a good lesson, and I've never forgotten it. Since I tried wine at a young age, when my friends invited me to go out drinking, it wasn't such a big deal. Like most Italians, my grandfather used to make his own wine and we always had it in the house. Unfortunately, my dad didn't take his own advice as he was a very big drinker.

When the holidays came around, it seemed harder to get over my loss and this was more enhanced by all the songs my grandmother loved. The mere fact I wasn't going to be able to be with her, after spending twenty-three years and holidays together, was more than I could possibly endure. I remember waking up on Christmas Eve morning. As Jim had to work, we weren't going to my parent's house for dinner that night. I was so heartsick. It hurt so badly, and I cried so hard that I vomited. It was one of the loneliest days of my life. I sulked in pain, knowing I wasn't going to enjoy our big traditional fish dinner together or be able to see all the beautifully wrapped gifts under the tree and the bright colorful shining lights on the decorated trees and houses. I just listened to songs that ripped my heart out, realizing I didn't have a grandma to hold me in her arms anymore. Somehow, I got through it with the help of God. I knew I had to go on—and go on I did.

The following year, I decided to try and find a job, but the commission was waiting for me to get a Seeing Eye dog. They thought I would be a good mentor, and helpful at teaching braille. I felt that's what God wanted me to do. So that spring, I called The Seeing Eye for a dog, and I was placed on their waiting list. They wouldn't take me until the following January, so I couldn't do anything but wait. That summer, on July twenty-sixth, I went to Hoboken with Jim and my mother to Saint Ann's Feast. She was the saint to pray to when asking for a baby. I walked in the procession with all the other ladies, and I was thrilled to carry the banner displaying her picture. In the procession was a float carrying the statue of Saint Ann where people could offer money that the men would pin to her robe. I was honored to carry the banner into the church that was reserved for only the president of the Saint Ann's Guild. I lit candles, prayed, and I waited.

In the fall of that year, I had an urge to go to The Basilica of Sainte Anne de Beaupre in Quebec, Canada. This was a shrine where Saint Ann had appeared to the sailors, and many miracles were performed in curing the sick and disabled. I had this strong yearning to go, so my husband agreed to take me. This was an eight-hour trip, and when my mom and dad heard that we were going, they wanted to come with us too. My mom told her sister, Angie. She and Uncle Tom also wanted to come. We all left on that Saturday as it was Columbus Day weekend, and Jim had Monday off. Jim drove halfway to Montreal, and we stopped there to see the Saint Joseph Shrine. My dad drove the rest of the way to Saint Ann's.

As we entered into the church area, I felt like I was walking into heaven. It was so quiet. The only thing you could hear were the nuns chanting, and it was so beautiful. I immediately went to the church and knelt in front of the statue of Saint Ann. As I did, my husband lit two candles—one for my sight, and the other for a baby. My mother and my aunt were praying very hard for my sight to be restored. Well, that didn't happen, and I know how hard it must have been on my family. At that point, I wanted to see, of course, but I also wanted to have a baby.

The next morning, we went to mass, and as I stood at the communion rail, I felt a hand on my shoulder. As we were leaving the church, a woman approached me, kissed me hello and said, "I will pray for you." My mother was in shock as this poor woman had cancer of the face, and she thought I would catch it. I guess you can see she didn't know too much about this disease, and when they looked around to see where she went, the woman had vanished. When I asked them who had put their hand on my shoulder, they just looked at me and said there wasn't anybody there. I felt that it was Saint Ann herself. It may sound crazy, but the circumstances surrounding this time, and afterward, brought me to that conclusion.

We walked over to the convent where the nuns lived, and took care of the visitors. We met this one nun, and my mom told her I wanted to have a baby, and to see again. She told her about my past misfortunes. The nun said she had something to give me. She left the room, and returned with a medal. On one side was Saint Ann, and on the other was Saint Gerard to whom you prayed to get pregnant. When she gave the medal to me, she said, "Tell me when you get pregnant." She didn't say, "Tell me if you become pregnant." The next day we left, and drove home by way of Maine as my father wanted to get real Maine lobsters. My poor husband drove all the way there, and all the way home. Going to Canada took about eight hours, but coming home took about ten. My father and uncle wanted to drive, but Jim just kept on going. When we arrived home, his eyes were so red. The poor man was so exhausted, he couldn't even go to work the next day. It was truly a labor of love and sacrifice for me, which would be just the beginning of many. Well, it was worth it as my feelings were right on. I received my miracle. That next month, I found out I was pregnant! Yes, miracles do happen!

Jay

On July 31, 1969, our son, Jay, was born. His birth name is James Gerard, named for obvious reasons. Everyone said he was a beautiful baby with a whole head of dark hair. I was so excited to finally have my baby, but it was so hard to put aside the heartbreak of not being able to see him. But I had my baby I was waiting for so long; and most of all, he was someone who needed me. I sent a note to that wonderful nun who gave me the medal. That wonderful woman gave me something more than just a medal; she gave me hope and faith in God and myself.

It wasn't hard for me to adjust to having a little baby, as I was so ready for one. All of my natural instincts fell into place. I was told by my counselor from the commission that I had to do everything myself so that the baby could bond with me. I nursed him, which was so much easier for me. My mom came to give me a hand, but I wouldn't let her do too much except hold or change his diapers as I was so intent on his bonding with me. She left after a week, knowing that I had everything under control, and was relieved that my sister was close by. I was so in love with my baby, and so happy that I had someone to care for. I needed to be needed. Doesn't everyone? I felt sad that I couldn't push him in his carriage alone, but my sister Rae helped me do it.

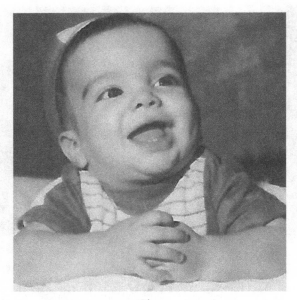

Glen

Two years later, on August seventeenth, we were blessed with another baby boy. We named him Glen Michael as I really liked the name and admired the astronaut, John Glenn, who was the first one to orbit the earth in a rocket. However, when I became pregnant with him, I couldn't understand how I could possibly love another baby in the same way I loved Jay. When I was giving birth, the doctor had to use forceps to remove him from the birth canal. My poor baby had marks on his temples, and was black and blue for a while. The poor kid looked like he went through a war. As soon as they put him in my arms, it was love at first meeting. Unfortunately, I can't say, "Love at first sight." He was a good baby, but Jay was very jealous. One day, I walked into the bedroom. I found Jay making his way toward Glen's crib. I went on to discover that Jay had a hat pin in his hand, and I'm pretty sure he was looking to stick it into Glen. Thank God I caught him in time, and they grew to get used to one another. Can I say it was easy? Not on your life, and it kept me very busy. And it was a good thing we were in a small apartment as well, since the boys couldn't go too far.

Having two children now forced me to muster up the courage to step up for my family who needed me. I came to this realization when Jim had just come home from the hospital after having surgery and couldn't go up and down the stairs as our apartment was above lower stores. Well, I did what I was used to doing by this time, went down to the deli, and bought a bottle of milk. When I realized what I had done, I stopped in the middle of the sidewalk, and exclaimed to myself and God, "I did it! My family needed me, and I came through for them!" I knew that now I could do anything with the help of God. I knew, after that day, He would always be walking with me. Nothing is impossible for God, not even a blind lady with a husband and two kids. I knew God heard me. But to answer my prayer exactly the way I saw it in my mind, and answer it the way I had asked, I was in such a state of euphoria that I just floated home the rest of the way. I don't know why I was in such shock as I had no doubt that God was for real, but with His help now, I was ready to face whatever life threw at me.

By this time, the apartment was getting pretty small, and the boys were getting big. When Jay was three, and Glen a year old, I prayed to buy a house. This seemed like an impossibility as Jim wasn't making too much money; and with a family and only one salary coming in, there wasn't any room for saving. He was working as a manager at a Shell service station in North Plainfield. Well, I started praying, and crying to God and the Blessed Mother about how much we needed a house. I prayed earnestly and specifically. I wanted to live in Chatham in a little house with a nice backyard for my boys to play. God says, "Ask and you shall receive."

I knew it wasn't going to be immediate, but I was willing to wait for God's perfect timing. Well this was the right time, and typical of the Lord and His works, he was right on! While Jim was recovering after surgery, he happened to go to the A&P Supermarket. Next to it was an abandoned Getty service station. On a sign was a phone number to call if anyone was interested in renting it. Jim came home so excited. He was going to try and rent it. Although we had nothing to go into business with, he was going to try anyway. Jim went for an interview, and they liked him right away as he had a great background and a lot of experience with service stations. After all, he was now already a manager at one. He went to the bank to get a loan, but he was denied because he didn't have any collateral. There was one bank, though, that did accept him. When they saw that he was never out of work, and never on unemployment or on welfare, the bank decided to take a chance. Now we had to get someone to co-sign the loan, and my sister and her husband came through for us.

The night before he was to take over the station, he was having reservations. I told him, "Don't worry. If you fail, you can always liquidate and get another job. Go for it. What do you have to lose? We have nothing now, so what's the difference?" The reason for feeling this way was that I had a lot of faith in Jim. He proved to me that he could do just about anything, so I didn't give it a second thought. These are the efforts that Jim showed me in the past, especially when he didn't have work or money. When the company he worked for laid him off, he went to work at the Shell station full-time until he could get better employment. We were so broke that we had to resort to food stamps for a short time, and my landlord was kind enough to accept late payment on the rent. Try doing that today!

Jim at the Getty station

On Labor Day that summer, while Jim was working at the station, I was watching Jerry Lewis on his annual telethon for muscular dystrophy. My heart went out to all those poor children, so I didn't think anything of it as I dialed and pledged three dollars. The next day, I mentioned it to my sister, and she thought I was crazy to do such a thing as we had so little money ourselves. This was true, but I just had to share the little we had. Soon after, I announced to her that I was going to have another baby. Well, I can't tell you how upset she was with me! She stormed out of my apartment, and I was left dumbfounded. When she returned, she apologized; but I must confess it really hurt me. Jim was then employed by Fedders Air Conditioning and Refrigeration Company, and that's when I gave birth to Glen. Soon after, he was offered a job as a manager at the Shell station in Plainfield. I'm sure you can see why I had no doubts that he could run a station. I felt my Jim could do anything he put his mind to. I was so thankful God was finally making his dreams come true. He deserved it. He was a wonderful provider, husband, and father.

Jim's Getty station

The next day, he went to his station with a mop and bucket in hand, and he got to work cleaning. In a few days, he was open for business. It turned out to be the best thing he ever did. Jim became very successful. Within six months, we were able to buy a little house in Chatham, and it had everything we ever wanted. We found the house in March, and Jim's sister, Anna, gave us a loan for a down payment, but we couldn't move in until the following October as the owners hadn't found a new house and wanted to sell theirs before doing so. That spring and summer was a long and frustrating time for me. I couldn't wait until my boys could play in their own backyard.

Jim's sister Anna and her husband George Northrup

When we moved in, my neighbor, Susie, came over with her little boy and said," Well, it's about time you moved in!" Her little boy
was as old as Glen and became fast friends as did we. We were in that
old apartment for almost nine years. Our families and friends were so
happy for us as they knew how much we wanted a house, and now
our dreams were finally coming true. The house was in such good
condition that we didn't have to do very much to it. With the help of
my mom, dad, and friends, we were all moved in and set up in one
weekend. It had only two bedrooms, but had a large dining room and
a nice-sized kitchen. The living room was small and all on one floor.
It also had a screened-in porch. My dad finished the basement for us,
and it was good that he did as my father-in-law came to live with us.

Jim's parents Jim and Rose Guzzi

Jim's sister Rose and her husband Jim Huelbig

Pop was down on his luck and had nowhere else to go. He lost everything through drinking and women. When Jim's mom died, he was only seventeen years old and his dad was drinking a lot, slowly lost his business, and eventually lost his two houses. His sister, Rose, and her family lived with him for many years, but he had to sell the house. So that meant she had to find somewhere else to live, and she was so angry at her dad that she left him to fend for himself. I couldn't blame her as he didn't give her any notice. She and her family came to live closer to us, and bought a house in Madison.

It was really difficult with Pop. He was always running back to Hoboken on the train, and Jim would have to go get him at all hours of the night, after putting in a twelve-hour day. When Pop came back on his own, he would be so drunk that he would mistakenly go into my neighbor's house. I must say it was quite embarrassing. He just couldn't adjust to living with us, and being away from Hoboken and all of his old cronies. The only way Jim could keep an eye on him was to take him to work with him at the gas station. But even there, Jim would take his eyes off of him and he would go missing. Well, we decided to hold his Social Security money. We would only give him a very small allowance, and he wouldn't have enough money to go anywhere. We used it to pay his bills, and his health insurance, but we never took anything for him staying with us.

Jim and his dad had a lot of arguments, and so did we. I hated for my boys to see their grandfather like that. How could I explain to them why he staggered or why he got sick? And we always had to clean it up! It was a very tough time for us, but he was Jim's dad and he had no one else to turn to. Jim's other sister, Anna, lived in a very small apartment with her family. I knew he needed us. I also knew he gave me a good husband, and I could never turn my back on him no matter how hard it was.

Just before Pop came to live with us, Jim won a trip to Bermuda. He won "Service Station of the Year" for having the cleanest of the older Getty stations in New Jersey. He was one of the winners along with ten other station owners. We were very happy about this. Before renting the station, when he was leaving his old job, Jim's former boss told him that he would never be able to keep up with it and all its problems. Well, we showed him! He was there at the award's dinner when Jim received his award, and he took a picture with Miss New Jersey. I was so proud of him that I thought I would burst. And I must admit I had to gloat over it with his old boss being there. It was nice to see him swallow his words.

Jim receiving "Service Station of the Year" award

Jim's Getty station interior

When I had to pack for our trip, I went up to our attic to get my summer clothes. As I was reaching to get my things, my foot slipped off the boards as the whole attic was not fully covered with flooring. I almost fell through the ceiling into our dining room, but I held onto the rafters as they caught me under my arms and held me. I didn't know whether I should pull myself up or jump down. Well, I thought if I jumped, I'd break my legs. So I pulled myself up. When I came down, Jay was coming home from school. When he saw the hole in the ceiling he said, "Dad is going to have a fit." I asked him if there was a big hole, and he confirmed there was. I called Jim, and the first thing he did was yell at me. He didn't ask me if I was all right. He was just concerned about the ceiling. I can't tell you how hurt I was that he didn't seem to care about me.

Later, he said, "Well, you were all right to talk on the phone so I figured you were fine." I did get hurt under my arms that were all bruised, but did he ask? No. That hurt me more than the bruises I had. Of course, he fixed the ceiling that same night as we were having all our neighbors over for a going away party—and did I get teased! All in all, we had a great trip even though it was only for a long weekend. When I got home, my neighbors couldn't wait to ask me if I had fallen through any ceilings lately. Ha ha!

The downside of owning a gas station at that time was the memorable gas shortage. It was terrible. People were in line with their cars for hours, and the lines were blocks long. This took place in the middle of the winter, and people were cold, tired, and angry. Some capitalized on it, however, as they would sell hot coffee, hot chocolate, and doughnuts. It was so difficult for mothers and their little kids, but good-hearted Jim would let them go to the front of the line. This upset the other customers who were waiting such a long time. People were allotted only so much gas, and you went on the odd or even day, according to your license plate number. People were so enraged that fights broke out in some stations, and Jim was almost shot when he would run out of gas. Yes, it was an awful time to be in the service station business. The price for gas was thirty-eight cents a gallon. It's ten times as much today.

Mark

Soon after, I gave birth to my third son, Mark. I really got to enjoy him. By this time, Glen was four years old, and Jay was six. I would have liked to have a little girl, but I was so happy. He was healthy and perfect. When Mark was about a month old, I was entertaining a couple of friends. I had Mark on the floor, and I was wearing an Italian horn around my neck. This symbol was to keep away evil spirits. I felt a tug on my neck, and the chain fell off. I began to get sick. So much so that I had to excuse myself and go to bed. I felt so sick that I thought I was going to die. I had a very high fever, and I thought I saw my grandmother at the foot of my bed. I thought she was coming for me. I told Jim, "I think I'm going to die." And, of course, he thought I was crazy, but I can't tell you the strong feeling I had. I felt like the angel of death was coming for me. I prayed for it to pass over me. Well, it did, and the next day I got a knock at the door. It was my neighbor's nephew asking if he could use my phone as he had been knocking on his aunt's door and she wasn't answering. His aunt was very old, so he was very concerned. He called her on the phone and didn't get an answer. He called the police, and they found her dead. She had died the night before. I still get chills when I think about that story. I took that horn and threw it out. I didn't need any symbols to keep me safe since I had God. I felt that the angel of death passed over me that night.

I really loved that house, and everyone else did too. A couple of my girlfriends had babies around the same time I did. They would come to my house, and we would all nurse our babies together while our older children would be playing outside in my backyard. All the kids liked to play at our house since we had all the toys and a swing set. I always had someone at my house during the day for coffee or just to chat. Sometimes, I got a little annoyed as I couldn't get my housework done. They didn't care about their homes like I did. But all in all, it was fun having friends to share all your thoughts and problems with. We had a lot of fun there and made lifelong friends.

One day, when Glen was about four years old, he was outside talking to our neighbor Bob. He asked Glen, "Can you tie your own shoes?" Glen proudly said, "No, but I can pour juice." My neighbor had the biggest laugh, and he always remembered it. He and Jay wanted to do things for themselves. So, I bought a narrow pitcher that they were able to hold and pour. Glen was very proud of himself.

Eight months later, after Mark was born, I found myself pregnant again, so we moved to a four-bedroom house in Florham Park. I was very unhappy about moving out of Chatham as I now had a lot of friends there, but we needed more room. Before I moved in, I thought I would never get used to living away from Chatham. You have to understand I knew Chatham and was used to it. I lost my sight there, and I knew all the streets. I knew nothing about this new town. I prayed to God to help me adjust, and He answered my prayers. The first day I moved in, one of my neighbors, Sue, brought a cake to us. She made me feel so welcome. The boys had a lot of neighborhood kids to play with. There must have been about twenty. In those days, you didn't have to make a playdate. You just went outside and you had all the friends you wanted. I soon realized I had everything I needed. I had my family.

I'm sure you must be wondering how I took care of all these children. When they were babies, like I said, I nursed them. But when they were older, and eating food, I sat them in an infant seat. I would place my left index finger next to their mouths, and p

45

the spoon into their parted lips. They would not open their mouths unless my finger was there, and if anyone else fed them, they had to do as I did. When they crawled, I put bells on their shoes. I had to put them in playpens to get any work done. Nowadays, moms don't do that. They don't want to confine their babies, which is so ridiculous. Smarten up, girls, and get a break!

When I took a walk with them, I would hold one of the kid's hands in mine, and with my other hand, I'd hold the other kid's hand along with my cane. When I bought clothes, I matched their shirts with their pants, so I always knew they matched. Then, when they got older, they could tell me what colors things were. As my children grew up, I gave them chores to do. My boys learned how to set the table, fill the dishwasher, dry pots—which I washed and wanted cleaned—and rinsed well. I didn't want to have soap bubbles in my next recipe. Later, they did other things like vacuuming, helping me clean the bathrooms, and they helped their dad with mowing the lawn and gardening. After they played with their toys, they always had to clean up. I taught them how to make their own beds, and pick up their clothes and put them into the hamper. I matched socks by feeling the tops, and matched underwear, shirts, and pants by size. My house was always neat and clean. That's how Jim and I were raised, and that's how my children would be also. Anyone could walk into my house at any time, and it was always in order. I could not have things around that I might trip on.

I am proud of the fact that if my children had any accidents, someone else was watching them. One time, I was in the kitchen at our apartment, and Jim was watching Jay who was only fourteen months old. Jay tripped on his own feet, hit his forehead on the edge of the coffee table, and got four stitches. As the boys grew older, they had a lot of falls, broken bones, and plenty of stitches. They were typical boys, and I was very used to running to the doctors with them. Mark was the worst as I think he had stitches on almost every part of his body. My boys were no pansies.

It never ceases to amaze me how God has you meet someone who would become a lifelong friend. Like the time after walking the boys to school for their first day, I was walking home, carrying Mark at sixteen months old, and I was very pregnant. A really lovely woman walked up to me and started a conversation. She saw how hard it was for me to carry Mark as he had gotten tired, so she asked me if she could carry him for me. I thought she seemed trustworthy, and I gave him to her—something you would never do today. We walked and talked, and I found out that she had a daughter in the same grade as Jay, and they lived up the street from me. Her name was Ginny. She and I became the best of friends. In those days, moms stayed at home to care for their children, and no one went to work. All my neighbors and I became good friends and helped each other.

Steven

On October 30, 1976, I gave birth to my fourth son, Steven. I couldn't believe I had another boy, but I was very happy to hold him in my arms, considering the problems and concerns he had given the doctors and nurses before his birth. He was in distress due to the umbilical cord being wrapped around his neck. The nurses were rolling me around to dislodge it, and thankfully they did. Doctor Bennett told me if they hadn't detected the problem, he could have choked to death at birth. I was so thankful. Another beautiful, healthy baby boy. My roommate's mother said to her daughter, thinking that I was asleep, "Poor thing. Another boy. Aren't you glad you had a girl after your two boys?"

My boys were funny. While still in the hospital they sent me some Halloween candy. They wanted to know if I ate chocolate while nursing the baby, would he get chocolate milk from me? When I brought Steven home, I felt not only did I have a full house, but a full heart. The Lord really gave me all I ever wanted. Yes, it would have been nice to have a little girl, but it wasn't meant to be.

I was really busy now with four boys. I didn't know what I was in for. I think having Mark at sixteen months old, and an infant, was far worse than having twins. When I was nursing Steven, Mark would be running around the house and climbing on the furniture. So, here I was with the baby in my arms, and running after Mark. I was so grateful to Ginny. If I needed her, she would come over. Sometimes, she would just happen to drop in. I think the good Lord sent her. At other times, she would take Mark to her house to give me a break. There was no doubt about it. It was tough, but I did it. I had to. What else could I do?

Soon after Steven was born, Jim had experienced pains in his chest and couldn't catch his breath. My dad ran him to the hospital. I was a wreck. I asked God, "You gave me all these children, and now you're going to take Jim away from me?" They took an X-ray, and it showed a blood clot next to his lung. The doctors put him on a heart monitor for a few days. Meanwhile, my church was having a charismatic renewal. Mom and I attended the services every night. This is when I accepted the Lord as my savior, the most important decision I had ever made in my life. I prayed so hard for a miracle, and not have Jim taken away from me. The three nights I went, this was all I thought of. Well, the next day, Jim was released and told there was a mistake with the X-rays. They were read wrong. It turned out to be a spot on the X-ray, and not his lung. At the time, we were going to a family practice where new doctors were learning and practicing. Well, they tried practicing on my husband, and I had enough of them. That was a mistake, and it could have been a fatal one. We went right back to my doctors at the Summit Medical group whom we originally left, because family practice was right in Chatham and close by. I know anyone can make a mistake, but not on my husband.

By accepting Jesus as my Lord and savior, I didn't realize exactly what I had done. It was in my head, and only lip service, but not in my heart. I called my sister and shared with her what I had just done. She was learning about the Lord too. She explained it to me, but I had to learn about my new friend myself. I know I had to read the Bible if I wanted to learn about Jesus. In a Catholic home, one didn't read the Bible. Only the priest did, and I had no clue. I remember, for one entire week, I was acting very nasty to Jim and my family, and I had no idea why. My sister Rae happened to come out for a visit, and I told her how I was acting. She said, "Now the devil is trying to get you back, and away from God." She said I needed to get some help learning about Jesus, and that I should go to a prayer group and Bible study. Well, I did just that.

The next Thursday night, I went to a prayer meeting at my church. When I walked in, the priest said to me, "Well, it's about time you came. I have been wondering when you would finally decide to come back here." After a while, Ginny invited me to go to her neighborhood Bible study that met every Tuesday between 12:00 p.m. and 2:30 p.m., just before the kids came home from school. We met at each other's homes. This Bible study group has been going on for the past thirty-eight years, and we are still going strong. My friend, Barbara Taylo, was one of the first people to start it. Many people have come and gone, but there are still eight of us that pray and study the Bible. I have been truly blessed with all these wonderful ladies, and our Bible study has been blessed by the Lord in keeping us together so long.

One evening, after prayer group, the priest gave me a Bible on cassette tapes. I was so thrilled, because now I would be able to study by myself, which I did every afternoon when the boys were taking their naps. I tried to learn about the word of God in any way I could. I would listen to Family Radio, which was a Christian station, and I really learned a lot. I learned not only things of the Bible, but other facts about raising a family in the Lord. I can't tell you what a help it was for me through the years. I also listened to the television and the televangelists on the 700 Club. Actually, this is when I really found the Lord.

One afternoon, after I put the boys down for their naps, I had the radio on. I was able to tune in television stations on this special radio I had. Obviously, I didn't have to sit and watch anything. I remember I was cleaning my kitchen after the boys had lunch, and I heard a man who was an artist tell Pat Robinson, the host, his testimony. I stopped what I was doing and listened. He was saying how he had so many burdens, and when he accepted Jesus into his heart, all his burdens were lifted off his shoulders. He said he felt light and free, and had someone to lean on and help him get through life. He didn't have to go it alone. He felt like a new person. It was so uplifting to me that I exclaimed, "That's what I want, too!"

I went into my dining room, got on my knees in front of my radio that was under the picture of the last supper, and I took Jesus into my heart. I said the sinner's prayer. "Jesus, I want you to come into my heart, please forgive me of my sins, and live your life in me. I want to make you Lord and master of my life." After that, I truly felt like my burdens were lifted, and I felt so different that I knew something wonderful had happened. I know it was the Holy Spirit coming into me. I felt new and clean. I really felt like a new creature in Christ. This was not lip service, but heart surrendering. I called one of the ladies from my Bible group right away. Jesus said, "If you confess me to others, I will confess you to my father in heaven." That whole day, I was singing and dancing around the house. It was truly a high—a high I have never come down from. As long as I have Jesus, I will never come down. Praise God!

Life was so different now for me and my family. I knew now what direction I had to take. I would follow Jesus, and so would my family. I tried my best to bring them to the Lord. We went to church every Sunday, and Sunday evenings after dinner, we would study the Bible with a study guide for young families. They said their prayers every night, and I prayed to God that they would take Jesus into their hearts, and make him Lord and master of their lives—which they eventually did. Jim came to the Lord when he heard a dynamic speaker talk about Jesus. At this time, I felt that we should go to a non-denominational church, but Jim thought we should stay in the Catholic church and raise our children in the faith we were raised into. He said if they wanted to change when they got older, it was their choice.

As time went on, our boys learned to love sports. The boys played baseball, football, and Steven played soccer. Jay also took piano lessons and did very well. At the age of 9, he played the piano in a recital. He played the Concerto in A minor, and it was perfect. I was so proud of him, along with Jim and my parents. I taped the whole thing, and he still has it to this day. Jay played the piano for a few more years, but as he grew older, he wanted to play the guitar and joined a band in high school. He did promise he would get back to the piano, because he knew how much I loved listening to him play. He kept his promise and now writes and records his own music. I think Glen felt like he was in Jay's shadow, and I was so glad when he played the trumpet. When our unwanted neighbors moved out, Glen marched in the middle of the street playing "When the Saints Go Marching In." These people were awful to the kids on the block. They didn't have any children and couldn't understand why they played in the street. They always called the police when our kid's baseballs and toys ended up on their property. So, it was no surprise that we were overjoyed when they left. Mark learned the saxophone, which lasted only about two weeks. He and Glen were my sportsmen. I loved to go and watch them play. Jim would take a break from work and bring me to a game. We would watch them for a little while. Then he had to get back to the station. Jay and Glen also bowled in a town league. In the summer, they went to day camp in town and stayed there from nine o'clock in the morning until three o'clock in the afternoon. Then, when they turned eleven years old, the boys could go to the town pool alone. I was lucky if I had someone to take me. That was a lot to ask of my neighbors. Jim and I would take them on Sundays when he was not working. I loved to swim, and my boys had to be taught as I was a fanatic about that. They all took lessons at the pool, but Jay and Glen learned how to swim at the YMCA. They learned in two weeks. I didn't want to wait, and had to be certain about their safety.

The boys rode their bikes everywhere. They just had to tell me where they were going, although I liked them to stay close to home where I could hear them. They played baseball in the backyard until they were too big and hit a ball that almost broke my neighbor's window. From that point on, they played at the many fields and parks in town. This is what I loved about Florham Park. There was always somewhere for the kids to play. There was the Tot Lot for the little ones, the schoolyards for the bigger kids, and a lot of baseball, football, and soccer fields in which to play. However, they loved just playing on the street in front of the house. All the kids were there, and they played stickball, Frisbee, rode bikes, and so many other games. Unfortunately, today you don't see much of that anymore. To have them around was great as I just had to call them for supper; or if they were up the block, I just rang my cow bell that hung on the side of my front door. When they heard that bell, they would call out, "We're coming!"

Our town has a great Jaycees organization that has different events all year round. At Easter time, they have the Easter Bunny riding on the top of a firetruck around town, and then an Easter egg hunt for all the children. On the Fourth of July, we have a parade and family fun, food, and games on the borough hall lawn. On Sunday nights, in the summer, they hold music performances at the town gazebo. When Halloween rolls around, they have a parade for all the kids in front of the middle school and give a prize to the best costume. On Christmas, Santa comes into town on a firetruck while they light the Christmas tree in the Gazebo. He sits them on his lap in the borough hall and listens to the kid's requests, and hands out hot chocolate. I was so blessed to be able to raise my children in this great town.

The boys did pretty well in school. They weren't scholars, but they did just fine with a lot of prompting. Like any other kid, they hated school. The boys would come home, I would give them a snack, and then they would do their homework. If they went out to play, and tried to do their homework after dinner, they would be too tired or want to watch television, which was a no-no. The school system was good, and I would pray all summer long for them to get teachers they liked; for if they didn't, I suffered all term. Florham Park had two grade schools and a middle school. We had to share the high school with East Hanover. It is called Hanover Park Regional High School. The boys took the school bus until they got their driver's licenses in their junior year. Sharing the high school kept our taxes down. We also had The Exxon Corporation as a good tax reduction. However, when Exxon left town, our taxes went up, but they were still a lot less than the surrounding towns.

Florham Park is very scenic with its trees and flowers. Beautiful pear trees surround our gazebo on a large, plush, green lawn. We don't have a Main Street, but a lot of mini malls. Florham Park is also known for its roller-skating rink and a recreation center for children. This also doubles as our senior center in the fall and winter, although we are now planning to build a new one. Our library is new as the old one was an original schoolhouse. It's called The Little Red School House and now belongs to The Historical Society. Florham Park was called Broom Town as it originally had a broom factory. Many years ago, it was mostly farmland with pastures, and now it has a beautiful park-like setting. It was owned by Florence and Hamilton, hence the name Florham Park. There's also a wonderful golf course at The Brooklake Country Club in town. We have many denominational churches, and we're located near all the larger malls. We can catch the train to New York just five minutes away in Madison—another great town to live—where we now attend Saint Vincent Martyr Church. Of course, I will have a fond regard for Chatham where Jim and I first started out. It holds bittersweet memories as it was fun being newlyweds, but that was the town where I lived when I lost my sight.

Speaking of newlyweds, I always wanted to keep our love alive in our marriage. Let's face it; when you have so many kids, your days are hectic. Jim worked long hours at the station and we were always so tired. But to keep the spark, I made sure I looked good when he came home. After all, he was with a lot of lady customers. I always gave him a kiss when he walked in the door and tried to ignore any crankiness. Dinner was always ready, while the boys were watching television. After dinner, and the boys were put in bed, it was our time together. Pop would be watching television or he'd just go into his room, and this was our time to talk over coffee. We would talk about the day's events and everything the boys did or didn't do. We would talk about our dreams and aspirations for the future.

Jim and I always kept the lines of communication open. This was very important for a good marriage, but at this time, our marriage was getting a little dull. The one thing that helped give my marriage a boost and spark it up was when I spoke to my best friend Ginny. She really took care of her husband, Sam. She would dote over him to the point where we thought she was a little too much. When Sam came home, he was treated like a king. Ginny didn't let him lift a finger if she could help it, and she did it all with her two daughters. When she mowed the lawn, we would call her "The Lawn Queen." One thing was definitely true: Sam was one happy man, and Ginny never complained about doing anything for him. She really enjoyed taking care of him.

I wanted to keep Jim happy, but I wasn't going to the extremes like Ginny. So one day I asked her what I could do to make Jim happier and spark up our marriage. This is when she told me about a book called *The Total Woman*. This book was very popular at the time. Luckily, I was able to get it from the Library for the Blind. I would listen to it every day after the kids went to school and as I went about my daily chores. It was a Christian book, yet the story seemed to be about a woman who was manipulating her husband; but it wasn't. The book was about advising women in many different ways, from changing your attitude and showing more affection toward your husband, to expressing love in your everyday life. For instance, in the evening, greeting him at the door wearing very little— which I never did, of course—or making him very happy when you were alone. It made you think of things to make him feel more like a man by using the Four "A" System: adore, affirm, affection, and admire. If you used all of these on your husband, he would be very happy.

Well, I did. It made a big difference, and I don't think Jim knew what hit him. By doing so, I was actually becoming happier myself, which was the whole premise and goal of the book. A happy wife makes a happy life for her man. There was a lot of scripture readings in it as well that backed it all up. One of the things I loved to do on a Saturday night was to have a fireside dinner in our family room, after the boys were in bed and Pop was in his room. We'd have a romantic dinner alongside the fire glow. For me, it was the crackle of the wood, the feel of the heat, and my imagination of the flames. Afterward, we would put on some music and slow dance, and then . . . well, you get the idea.

If I was lucky, my mom and dad would come over and watch the boys so we could get away alone together for a weekend. We would go up to The Pocono Mountains or down to the shore. We did this once a year. We felt we needed it for the good of our marriage. These times were wonderful, just being alone with each other and not having the kids around for a little while. It was only the two of us and no one else. I felt like we were the only people in the world. I must admit, I didn't really need a book to tell me what to do as Jim and I had a lot of loving before that. After all, wasn't it obvious? Look at how many kids we had! Well, after a while, the inevitable happened. After all that loving, I was pregnant again—and then came the real shock.

One Tuesday, at Bible study, my friend Mary Lou who had ten children herself asked me, "Bea are you pregnant?"

I asked, "Why, do I look like I am?"

She said, "Yes, in fact, you look like you're having twins." I hadn't gone to the doctor yet, but at that time, I didn't want to say anything as I didn't know for sure. I remember on Easter Saturday I was making Easter bread after enjoying being with the boys at the opening day of baseball. I was kneading the dough and thinking about how it was going to be with another baby, and what the boys would say. That night, for our anniversary, Jim took me to dinner at The West Orange Manor, one of the most exclusive restaurants in Jersey. I must admit I was a little apprehensive about having another baby.

Many things were going through my mind. But when we went in Jim's antique Cadillac, and I was wearing my fur jacket and my best jewelry, I thought to myself, "God has blessed us so much, and now he is giving us another blessing." As we passed the office where they plan the weddings, I thought maybe it would be a girl this time. And that's when I started praying for one.

Unfortunately, at the time, the business wasn't doing too well. The rent went up, and Jim couldn't keep up with the quota of gas the company wanted him to sell. In order to meet it, he had to come up with the money himself. Also, the company had changed hands and the new oil company didn't care about people—only money. Things were getting tough. So here I was pregnant again, already with a big family, and Pop. Of course, I started praying for the Lord to help us out of this. I always felt a baby brings blessings, and we certainly needed some now. The Bible reads, "Whoever welcomes one of these little children in my name welcomes me" (Mark 9:37, NIV). I hung onto that verse to get me through, but what happened next was beyond shocking—it was unbelievable. I truly felt the power of the Lord, and He helped me through the next part of my life. What I had to face was going to take a lot of strength and courage, but I had to do it. There was no turning back now. There was nothing else I could do about it, so I faced it head on.

It was the spring of 1981. I was expecting again, and having four very active boys, a large family is hard enough for anyone to handle. But for me it was even harder being completely blind. I was really glad I had a lot of experience with children since I always helped babysit my twelve cousins. At that time, I was sighted, had a lot of faith, and felt in my heart that if God gave me another baby, I would be okay. I thought my childbearing days were over, but God had other plans for me. Now five years later, I found myself pregnant again.

I was just starting to get used to having a little time for myself as my youngest son Steven was in nursery school three mornings a week and was going to start kindergarten in the fall. It was nice to be able to take a shower in peace, talk on the phone without any interruptions, and actually finish cleaning the house before the boys got home from school. Then I helped them with their homework, cooked dinner, made their lunches for the following day, and got them all ready for bed. So, you can imagine I wasn't too thrilled about starting all over again, but I was in store for the shock of my life.

When I went to my doctor's office for my second visit, I got the biggest surprise. I was in awe when Doctor Bennett said to me, "Bea, I think you're having twins."

I replied, "That's not funny, Doctor." But he wasn't joking.

Soon after, he went to my husband Jim's gas station in Madison and said to him, "I hope I'm wrong for Bea's sake." By my fifth visit to his office, he told me to go for a sonogram to find out for sure. I did and it showed two babies. By this time, I was actually getting used to the idea of having twins. I thought back to the time when I begged God to have a baby after being married for five years and being unsuccessful in having one. I was thinking back to the time of my plea to God and my determination to have a baby. I felt very guilty about being so selfish about having twins, so I asked for his forgiveness. "Delight yourself also in the Lord, and he will give you the desires of your heart" (Psalm 37:4, NIV).

Jim was very upset for me. He would ask me, "How are you going to do it? It is one thing having one baby, but quite another having twins."

I replied, "If God has enough confidence in me, who am I to question him? Besides, I can do all things through Christ who strengthens me" (Philippians 4:13).

He was also concerned about our financial situation. He would question how we would support two more children, and where we would have room in our house for them along with Pop who was still living with us. Jim was very concerned since he was going to be the sole provider for nine people. With much confidence, I told Jim, "There's always room for one or two more. God will provide." Jim's concern was how he would support all of us when the twins were born, yet my concern was for my babies to have sight and not inherit my horrible disease. I prayed on my knees each day and had great faith they would be fine as my boys were.

Of course, I also hoped for a little girl. I could picture her with bows in her hair, wearing a fluffy pink dress, and wearing little Mary Jane shoes. She would play with her dolls and a tea set—that would be so different than baseballs and trucks. "At least one girl," I'd cry as I didn't want to be greedy. Back then, doctors couldn't tell what you were having, so I prayed extremely hard. I just couldn't see myself having six boys. If it were to happen, I would still love them all the same; although I may have to be put on Valium. Can you imagine twin boys at the age of two?

Well, the big day came. I was at home having our weekly neighborhood Bible study when I started having contractions. I was six weeks early. It was normal for twins. When I was about to leave, my son, Glen, who was in the fifth grade asked me, "Aren't you coming to my school for Back to School night?" I felt bad as I had never missed one Back to School night or any after for that matter, but the babies had to come first. It was just like in the movies. Jim was speeding down the road when a policeman stopped us. He came over to our car, and Jim said, "I have to get to the hospital, my wife is having twins!"

The policeman nervously said, "Follow me!" When I got there, I didn't give birth until the next afternoon. The nurse that took care of me when I had first entered the hospital the night before came into the labor room for her next shift the following day, and she could not believe I was still there. Finally, at about one o'clock, they gave me an epidural to numb the pain. This was good since giving birth naturally was not for me. When the nurses rolled me into the delivery room, Jim was at my side just as he was with every one of the boys. He said, "Don't worry, honey, if they're boys, we'll love them just the same." I knew he was trying to soften the blow if they weren't girls, but I kept the faith and hope alive in my heart. As I was being settled on the table, the doctor told me he had some interns observing the multiple deliveries. So, there I was with all of these people staring at me. I was a little embarrassed, but so anxious I didn't care who was there at that point.

My heart was pounding, my mouth was dry, and I was holding my breath silently praying, "Dear Lord, let it be a girl. Please, just one." Then I heard the words I prayed for.

"It's a girl! It's a girl, Bea!" said Doctor Bennett. I thought I was dreaming. I had heard those words in my dreams so many times before, and now it was really true. I was so thrilled, I raised my hands up and said, "Praise the Lord, and thank you, Jesus!" God gave me what I had asked for. Ask and you shall receive.

Then six minutes later, the doctor shouted, "Bea, it's another girl!" I couldn't believe it! Two girls! Jim and I held hands and just cried.

Gayle

Jean

"She's our bonus baby," we said. When they placed the girls in my arms, it was the most wonderful feeling I ever had. Even though I couldn't see them, I was actually holding my answered prayers. I felt their faces and their bodies. They were perfect to me. The girls were fraternal twins, and everyone told me they were beautiful. I knew they were because I could see them with my heart. After the babies were checked over by my pediatrician, he quickly informed me the babies were fine and that their retinas were perfect. God doesn't answer prayers halfway, but all the way! As I held them close to me, I thought to myself, *I kept the faith.* "Now faith is the substance of things hoped for, the evidence of things not seen" (Hebrews 11:1, KJV).

When word got out that I had twins, I received many gifts and phone calls. My mother took care of the boys at home and kept me updated on their activities. They couldn't wait until I brought the babies home. Everyone was so happy for us. At Jim's gas station, one of his customers who was a florist placed big pink bows on Jim's gas pumps. It had a big sign that read, "Twin girls," and Jim placed it in his window with their names, date of birth, and weights on it. The funny thing about it was the smaller sign next to it which read, "Help Wanted" as he was looking for a new gas attendant.

As time went on, I soon learned I could've used the help too. I was unable to bring the girls home as they were premature and too small. My friends and neighbors would bring me to the hospital in the afternoon to nurse them, and Jim would bring my milk at night. The nurses called him the milkman. Gayle weighed five pounds and one ounce, and Jean weighed four pounds and one ounce. They dropped in weight and couldn't be brought home until they reached five pounds.

One week later, I brought Gayle home and had her all to myself. My mom went home. Two weeks later, Jean came home, and I'll never forget when the boys walked in. They saw I had them sitting in their infant seats on the kitchen table dressed in pink dresses and bows in their hair. The cameras came out and this was just the beginning of many pictures to come.

Besides taking care of the kids, there was enough to do around the house. Jim hired a housekeeper to help me with the heavy work for about two months. I never had a housekeeper before and never did after. Things were getting tight financially, so we couldn't keep her as well as many other things. Jay's piano lessons were the next to go. He wasn't too upset since he started to learn the guitar, but he promised to take piano lessons in the future. He did keep this promise. He still plays to this day and has written and recorded his own album.

Food shopping became very costly for the amount of people in the house, so the garden Jim and the boys planted the previous spring was a big help. I froze the vegetables, and made a lot of tomato sauce that summer. I was so glad I knew how to make something with very little. I went back to making peasant meals as we used to call them when we were first married. I would make greens and beans, pasta dishes, and bone soup as my boys fondly called it. Bone soup was a chicken broth made up of bones from the frame of the chicken and vegetables that we had eaten the night before. Hence the name bone soup. I took pride on being the gourmet leftover chef.

The boys had to pitch in and help with all of the chores when they got home from school. With the babies getting up every two hours, to say I was tired was an understatement. Everyday went into the next, and I never knew when the last left off or when the new day began. I was in a constant fog. One night as I tried to get some rest, I prayed, "Dear Lord, I don't know how long I can go on like this. Please help me. I'm exhausted." The next day, my friend Barbara called. She was one of the girls who had started our Bible group many years before I had joined. She also had six children and knew precisely what I was going through. After hearing my weary voice, she suggested that I get the names of all the people who had called and offered to help me. Many friends and neighbors did call to see how I was doing or just out of pure curiosity.

I did what she advised and she lined up ladies to come and help me one hour each day. They came and brought dinner or would help by feeding a bottle to one baby while I nursed the other. Sometimes, they would fold my laundry or let me lay down to rest. Some would just sit and have a cup of tea with me so I could have some adult conversation. What a great help they were!

Bible group

My other friends from my Bible study group really helped me out as well. My friend, Sue, would come and stay with the girls every Tuesday, while my other friend, Ginny, took me to Bible study. This was a great blessing to get out of the house for a couple of hours a week. They became the girl's godmothers. Another wonderful friend, Connie, would give Jim and me a break by doing our grocery shopping every week after she did her own shopping for her family. One Sunday, my oldest friend, Aggie, even stayed with the girls so we could have a family outing. Of course, others would just call to give me advice or just to talk, which is something my friend, Sharon, would do. My mom lived about an hour away and didn't drive, so she couldn't help much. And the rest of my family lived out of state. Jim's sisters lived closer, but they worked, and had families of their own. At times, they would visit on the weekends. The Bible reads, "Ask your neighbors next door for help before calling on your family far away." The Lord truly blessed me. "Never will I leave you. Never will I forsake you" (Hebrews 13:5, NIV). His presence was certainly evident then.

One day, I received a phone call from The Mothers of Twins Club and was asked if I would like to participate in sharing or exchanging different items necessary for twins. I agreed and thanked them for calling. Although I was very blessed to have everything I needed, my friends and neighbors gave me a baby shower. I really didn't think of the club much after that, but they called sometime later and announced to me that they had chosen me to be that year's "Mother of the Year." I was surprised, because I felt I had not done anything more than any other mother of twins was doing. They informed me that they would be coming by to give me something. I thanked them and hung up the phone.

I thought I would be receiving a plaque or a nice bouquet of flowers or something small. Well, the Monday before Thanksgiving, Jim and I prepared a Thanksgiving basket of food for a family in need at our parish Saint Vincent Martyr. We didn't have much, but we could certainly share what we did have with others. Jim had just left our house with the basket when someone rang my doorbell. I opened the door, and a sweet woman told me she was from The Mothers of Twins Club, and she had something for me. An army of people walked in and brought in all kinds of goodies for us. They stocked my cabinets, my pantry, my refrigerator, my freezer, and even more was overflowing onto my countertops and kitchen table! I thanked them and thought to myself, *I still have enough to share with others.* It goes to show that you can never outdo the Lord. "Give and it will be given to you. A good measure, pressed down, shaken together, and running over, will be poured into your lap. For with the measure you use, it will be measured to you" (Luke 6:38, ESV).

Bible group 2018

When Christmas rolled around, many friends helping me were from Saint Patrick's Church in Chatham, the church we attended when we were first married. These wonderful ladies brought us food, and toys for our children. I was so humbled by their generosity. I fell on my knees and thanked God for his marvelous abundance. "How priceless is your unfailing love, O God" (Psalms 36:7, NKJV)! I had to do something to repay everyone for their amazing outpouring of help and such unselfish love toward me and my family. So on a beautiful day in June the following year, I hosted a luncheon for all the ladies who helped me. The girls at eight months old were finally sleeping through the night, so I felt like a normal person again.

The Lord blessed me with forty wonderful helpers. As I said grace, I had such a feeling of gratitude sweep over me. "And my God will meet all your needs according to the riches of His glory in Christ Jesus" (Philippians 4:19). And He did! I had so much faith and trust in the Lord. By Him having faith and trust in me even though I was blind, it was the encouragement I needed to go on. I am so thankful to God for bestowing the honor and opportunity to raise His little ones.

I must say I really enjoyed my girls, but it was doubly hard with the two of them wanting me at the same time. I did my best to give them equal time; or I should say they demanded equal time. I had to feed them at the same time when I finally weened them. I nursed them for eleven months. From six months on, I started giving them table food. So by the time they could eat food, they had a head start. I would go back and forth from one to the other. It was a little easier when Jim was home and could help. He didn't have too much patience, especially when they would spit out their food all over the highchairs, getting it in their ears and hair. He would get angry at me for making such a mess, but I would get sassy with him and tell him to try doing it with his eyes closed. The problem was I didn't look blind, and he would forget. Well, you can imagine I taught them how to eat by themselves pretty fast.

To get anything done in the house, I would put them in their playpens. I had two and set them in the middle of the living room. I was always in the kitchen more times than none, so I could hear them close by. They played with their toys and sometimes hit each other with them. One day, my friend Aggie was visiting and she noticed that the girls would reach across the play pens and touch their index fingers together. They held them there for a few seconds. I think they did that to feel close. I was so glad she had seen that, because I would never have known they were doing something so precious.

I always put them in dresses, but in pants when it was cold. The girls wore bows in their hair, and I loved dressing them up. They were like two baby dolls. I also put bells on their shoes so I could hear them wherever they were. We didn't put any fences up by the stairs, because I was afraid I might forget when carrying the girls down and fall over them. So, they learned how to crawl up the steps and slide down. As they grew older, the girls would hold onto the railings and walk down.

The boys had a lot of fun with them, and they were a big help for me. When they came home from school, the girls would wake right up from their naps when they heard their brothers since they weren't too quiet. The boys would make them laugh and they loved to hear them giggle. All the boys were a big help, and Jay and Glen would change the girl's diapers for me but mostly if they were only wet. When I was cooking, the boys helped keep the girls occupied. But when their friends came, they were very eager to run outside and play. All in all, they helped me a great deal.

The Lord knew I would need help, and my boys were my extra hands. My best helper was Steven. At the age of five, he was always around and loved to take control. I think he wanted to feel like the big brother to the girls when his big brothers weren't there. Steven would watch them for me while I went to the basement to do laundry or other chores. I would never leave them unattended when they weren't in their playpens. I didn't like to keep the girls in them too long, because they needed to get around and explore. And explore they certainly did!

I never took any chances. I had locks on the cabinets, and would never leave them alone on a bed or the changing table to run for something. I had to think of everything and cover all the bases. I had this rule with all my children. Another thing I never did was leave the kids in the tub to answer the phone or anything else. It could wait. My babies came first!

Of course, accidents can happen. You can't have your eyes on them constantly. Like any child, they got hurt playing when they were older. They fell or would skid off their bikes or go into a tree with their sleds. You know, the usual kid stuff. They would come home crying and show me where the cut was, and I would feel the blood coming out. I knew it was blood because blood is sticky, and a bruise was a lump. They never wanted me to touch it, but that was too bad. I had to.

The only child to get hurt in my care was Glen. I happened to be talking to a young babysitter. She was about to leave, and the boys were jumping from the top of the steps down to the bottom. I told them to stop and as I said it, Glen came down, hit his eye on the edge of the piano, and split his eye lid. We rushed him to the Summit Medical Group and he got stitches. I was so thankful his eye was not hurt. That was the only time my child was hurt in my care. I felt awful because it was one time too many.

The girls weren't as bad as the boys, except when Jean received four stitches on her forehead. Jim and I were at my friend Barbara's anniversary party. It happened to be at the squad house where she was a member. When the alarm went off, for some reason I had a sinking feeling it was one of my kids, and I was right. Jean was playing in the backyard with her brothers and sister. She tripped and fell, and hit her head on one of the stones we had surrounding a bird bath. Grandpa was watching them at the time. We rushed her to the medical group where we met a surgeon on call. He took one look at her and called a plastic surgeon. He told him to get right down because, "We have a real cutie here." Thank God a plastic surgeon was still there. She had a scar, but as she grew, the scar became less noticeable. Many years later, the girls were sleigh riding with their brothers. Gayle was sliding down the hill with Jay. She went into a snow bank, and hit her chin on some ice. Well, she got a couple of stitches; and thank God, they too faded in time.

Yes, it was a noisy, busy, sometimes crazy house. But you know what? I loved every minute of it! Even when the girls were crying to be changed or to be fed, and the boys were running around the house after each other, fighting about Jay changing something on the television that they were watching or who wouldn't share what they were eating, I had to step in and be the referee. I tried to be fair, but at times it was hard. One would cry, then he'd get fresh, and he would end up punished in his room. At that time, there weren't any televisions in the bedrooms, no computers, and no radios. They just had books or their Speak and Spell and Pacman. These were battery operated, handheld games that would occupy them and give me a break. Well, at least for a little while. My famous sentence was, "Wait until your father gets home." If it was something bad, I'd tell him; but more times than not, I wouldn't. They were in my care, so I enforced the disciplining.

When Jim was home, I was more than happy to leave that job in his hands. Besides, if I called him about something the boys were doing or had done, he would inevitably say, "Put them in their rooms." What he didn't realize was after a short time, they would be pleading to come out. I didn't know which was worse: having them nag me to come down or letting them fight it out themselves. As they grew older, that's exactly what I did, and I kept out of it. Yes, I must admit, I wanted to run away and hide. It was easier to discipline them when they were small, and I tried to let the punishment fit the crime. If it wasn't that bad, I would talk to them and give them one more chance or send them to their rooms. It had to be really bad for me to spank them or take away something they loved to do or play with. Yes, I said spank, which I did when needed. I was the one in command, and they had to obey or else!

I had to be firm at times or I knew they would try to walk all over me. They knew I meant what I said, and said what I meant. I would tell them, "Don't let me say it. You know I'll do it." I would never let them get the upper hand. I taught them to listen and to be respectful. I always had them apologize to me or whoever they hurt or bothered. Jim, on the other hand, would throw the book at them for something very small. Then when he punished them, I wondered who was getting punished: them or me! For instance, he'd take their bikes away or not let them watch television for a week. Good Lord! Give me a break! He went off to work, and then there I was to carry out the punishments. They may have been punished, but I suffered! So that is why I took things into my own hands when he wasn't home. But when he was home, and they did something wrong, I would cringe when he would give a punishment. It was out of anger at times, and he was fast with his hands. Where he could reach, that's where they got it. It was one thing if I spanked them, but I didn't like them to be hit by a strong, and more powerful man. I felt he could really hurt them, but most of the time he did put the fear of God in them.

The boys loved him, but were afraid of him. He gained respect, but I don't think the boys ever felt that they could get close. Jim meant well and thought he was doing the right thing in his way of discipline. After all, that's how we were raised. Even though Jim's dad gave him everything, he was hit plenty and was spoiled. I wasn't raising my children that way. Jim had other ideas about how to raise children, and that's the way he was taught. We argued about this often. My girls, on the other hand, were spanked if needed by Jim on their butts, but I never did. I just had to raise my voice and they listened. Unfortunately, it was different with the boys. Of course, they would all try my patience and see how far they could get. Well, not too far! Unfortunately, Jim would preach and not just sit down and talk. He just didn't know how to listen. He would yell, the kids would get upset and go crying into their rooms. I was always the middleman. I would go up to their room and try to explain their father's point of view. Then I would go back down and plead the child's side. Jim would always say, "Sure, baby them." For whatever it was worth, I tried to have a happy and congenial home. It was not easy! Jim was soft-hearted, and I knew I could get around him. Eventually, he would come around and see my side.

Jim is a great husband and a devoted father. I have a lot of love and respect for him. He's very generous, and always tries to do the best for his family. He's a very dependable person and a wonderful provider. The kids had a fatherly relationship with him, but not as a buddy. Through the years, too many harsh words were said, and unfortunately, could never be forgotten. I regret to say these words stayed with them all their lives. However, they get along and love him anyway. Let's face it: who's perfect? The only thing you can do in life is try to do your best. We raised them the same way we were raised. We taught them to love God and to fear the loss of Him. Jim and I tried to teach our children to respect us, themselves, and authority.

Being a very positive person, I tried to build them up when they were feeling down about themselves, and to bring out their good points. After all, everyone needs to hear they are better in something than someone else. For instance, Jay is great at playing the piano and guitar, and for Glen, it is cooking and sports. Mark excelled at playing sports, especially baseball, and has the best sense of humor. Steven can build or fix anything he puts his hands on. Gayle was a great dancer, and danced for thirteen years until her high school graduation. She is very organized and dependable. Jean was great at soccer and was on the varsity team all four years of high school, and she is great in art.

As the kids grew up, I tried to create as many fond memories as I possibly could. In the winter, we took them sleigh riding down the hill in Madison or ice-skating on Sunrise Lake in Morristown. When Jay and Glen were four and two, we went up to my brother Carl's house, and the kids ice-skated on his pond with their cousins and their neighborhood friends. On the way home, at about eleven o'clock at night, Jim drove into an ice rut, and we had a very bad accident hitting a telephone pole. The 1964 Chevy convertible was totaled. Jay was sitting in the middle while Glen was on my lap. Jim's head hit the steering wheel, Jay hit his mouth on the dashboard and pushed his teeth up into his gums, my head went through the windshield, but Glen was fine. My arms held him back like a seatbelt. In those years, there weren't any seatbelts or car seats for children. Now I know first-hand how important these things are in a car.

God was truly with us as we had just passed a reservoir on the right side, and a mountain on our left. No one was around at that time of night, but just one car. Luckily, there was a phone booth right across the road. A man called the First Aid Squad and my brother. Needless to say, he couldn't get to us fast enough. Jim stayed in the hospital overnight. The areas by my eyebrows had to be stitched. The doctor told us Jay's teeth would eventually come down by themselves, and thank God, Glen was fine. My brother thought I was really out of it when I said, "Did I ruin my make up?" I knew he was pretty upset, so I had to use my sense of humor on him, but he didn't think it was too funny. My parents lived in the area too. When they came and saw a cover over my face, they thought the worst. They didn't know at the time, the doctor was getting ready to stitch me up. My mom and dad were happy to see I was going to be fine. This was not such a great memory. However, I appreciated that I was going to be thirty the coming April, a birthday I was dreading. I'll tell you right now, I was never so happy to reach that birthday!

I had to take every opportunity to get out with the boys when Jim was able to get away from the station. When Mark was still an infant, about one month old, I packed him in his front carrier and I tied him in front of me. It was like a kangaroo pouch. We took the boys to Wild West City. Jay and Glen loved it, but Mark slept through the whole thing. We also took them to the zoo, had picnics in Lewis Morris Park in Morristown, and of course, we went to Saint Ann's Feast in July. I will always honor the saint who prayed for me to have children. We also went to a lot of festivals and carnivals. When the girls came along, it was a little harder to get out, but we managed. I had to take doubles of everything, and just going to the mall was a big deal. Poor Jim had to push a double carriage with me holding on, and tried to watch where the boys would wander off to. Those were the times when we had to get clothes and shoes for all of them. What a job that was! I personally loved it since I was able to get out of the house, but I'm sure Jim couldn't wait to go home. Yes, it was tough, but we did it.

When the girls were almost a year old, my friend Aggie watched them for us so we could give the boys some of our attention. The girls were getting plenty of it at the time, and they were very demanding. So we took the boys to the Flemington Fair where they saw the largest vegetables grown in the area, all the local animals, and a stock car race that, being boys, they really enjoyed. *Fast* is their middle name, which ranks right up there with *cars*, and we had a great day.

Another time, Aggie and Barb took my girls to their houses for a long weekend. Jim and I took the boys to Disney World on the Napa Auto Parts tools promotion. It was an all-inclusive paid trip, so how could we resist? We had a great time, especially since it was our anniversary. God truly blessed me with the best of friends. The Lord will supply all our needs, and He surely did!

I think what the children enjoyed the most were the summers at the Jersey shore. We would take a long weekend and go to Wildwood Crest for about five days, because it was difficult for Jim to get away from the station for a whole week. We stayed at hotels on the beach. Some were nice, and some years they were not so nice. At that time, one couldn't go on the Internet to see what they were like. Jim had a phonebook and would call to see if there were any vacancies. As usual, we would wait until the last minute when it was close to the end of the summer, but we were so happy to get away. Pop came with us too, but as he became older, he didn't want to bother coming. Jim's sister, Rose, would have him stay at her house in Madison. He would go to the station every morning and back to her house at night.

One time, when Pop did come with us, we stayed at The Waikiki. He called it The Wacky Wacky as this was not one of the good ones. When we walked into the back room, there were dead flies all over the floor. The boys thought this was great. Those are boys for you! We cleaned them up and made the best of it. After all, we weren't in the room all that much. We had the boys in the ocean, in the pool, and we went on bike rides. Jim and I would ride a tandem bike and loved riding. I would bring dinners from home, and one night we took them on the boardwalk to eat and go on the rides. Jim and I would save the last night to take them out to a family restaurant. On the morning of our departure, we would go to our favorite place for breakfast, The Captain's Table. The very last thing we did was ride go-karts before heading home.

In the summer, after we had gone to Disney, we took the girls down the shore to Wildwood. I knew I would need help, so I invited my Auntie Jo to come with us. She was not related to me but was a very close friend of my family. She was in her late sixties, but she was very active. She loved children, and worked in the Morristown school system as a baker. Auntie had three sons who were not living at home any longer. She would take the train to Madison, walk to Jim's station, and he would drive her to our house. She would always bring cookies that were huge. My boys loved her and her cookies. She was a big help to me and Jim at the shore. Can you imagine lugging all that stuff down to the ocean? We had the playpen, the toys, all the towels, and anything else the boys could think of bringing. Jim felt like he was a packed donkey. Inevitably, someone had to go to the bathroom as soon as we got down there. How Jim didn't run away or drown himself, I'll never know. Now that's true love! I think Jim was always more than happy to get back to work. I wasn't too happy about going home as I really enjoyed the change, although they did have the town pool to go to. Of course, I looked forward to school opening. Yay! Hang out the flag!

We tried to make them happy with their different requests. For instance, Steven wanted a dog. Now, come on, did I really need something else to clean up after? My girls had just gotten out of diapers. Hooray! That was a monumental moment. One day, Steven brought home two ducklings from his classroom for the weekend. When the girls saw them, they jumped up onto the picnic table and screamed in fear of them. But as the weekend wore on, the girls got used to the cute little creatures. What I saw was how Steven took such good care of them. He was in the fourth grade at the time. His teacher, Mrs. D'Amico, just knew he was very responsible. And she was right. So I gave in and we bought a little Maltese. He was white and fluffy, so I named him Puffy. Of course, the boys wanted to name him Killer, but he didn't look anything like one. Steven was good with him, but I had to do all the training. I was a little experienced since I had a few dogs when I was younger. The only pets they had were the goldfish we'd get from the festivals, but they never lasted too long. When we'd find them floating on top of the fish bowl, we'd send them back to sea and right down the toilet. So that's why they wanted something that would live a little longer than just a few days.

As they grew older and into their teens, the boys got jobs at the age of fourteen. I thought that was a good age for them to start seeing what it was like to earn money and save. Jay and Glen worked at the gas station with Jim. They would come home from school, and ride their bikes to Madison; something you can't have your children do today. When Mark was of age, he worked at a station in town, and Steven worked at McDonald's. The girls babysat, but didn't like it, so they worked at Cullins Fresh Foods store in town. They all had a job. When Jay and Glen got their driver's licenses, they delivered pizza, and Mark and Steven did the same. They all had to juggle their time between school and work, but they did it. After all, they had to support their cars. Being in the business, Jim found them their first cars.

They were usually older vehicles, but they all ran well. He bought them, but they had to pay the insurance. They were hard workers and soon learned the value of a dollar. But being kids, they blew a lot of it, even though I tried to enforce saving. Some were saving their money, and others liked spending it. I knew they would learn for themselves.

After Pop passed away in 1985, I decided to get a job. The reason was obvious: we needed the money because Jim was having a hard time with the station and the Getty Company. Also, I had to prove to him that I could get a job. One day, when we were in a heated argument, I told him I was going to get a job. He had the audacity to say to me, "Oh, sure, what can you do? Just babysit?" Well, I had to show him that I was capable of doing anything I put my mind to! So I called The Commission of the Blind, and they helped me get a job as an answering service for the U-Haul trucking company two nights a week. It was difficult staying up all night, taking care of people who had problems with their trucks, and finding a garage in their area that was open. I used braille books to help find the proper service garages, and I had to page the person who was on call that night. I also had a double phone connection: one for me, and the other connected to a recorder to give the correct information to the garage. Sometimes, I couldn't get someone to help them, and they became very angry.

After working for a while, I felt like they just used us so the people had someone to complain to until the morning when they would send out their own mechanics. They used us through the spring and summer, and then laid us off. There were about six blind people that worked for them. I thought they pulled a lousy trick on us, because we couldn't get unemployment benefits since we didn't work more than seventeen weeks. I didn't care about that for myself, but I did for all the other people since they needed the money. My need wasn't as extreme as theirs. I was happy for the experience, because I thought I would be able to use it for the future. I must admit, it was sweet to be able to give Jim my first check, and I told him to use it for himself. He was embarrassed and hated to see me up all night working, and then the next day take care of everyone. But I did it and was mighty happy that I could. At the end of that summer, I had saved enough money to take my family down the shore. Yes, every experience you have in life is a stepping stone into your future. You never know how God will use it, and He did!

Soon Jim sold the station and went into the painting business. The kids were getting bigger and we needed more room. We were going to put on an addition, but I couldn't think of being without a kitchen for God knows how long. In 1988, we decided to buy another house in town. I found my dream house on Murphy Circle: a four-bedroom colonial with woods in the back. The house was on the inside of the circle and had a big backyard. The kitchen was huge, the middle school was around the corner, and a block away was the pool, ball fields, and library. This was a great spot for me since I couldn't drive, and the kids could get around by themselves on their bikes.

The Guzzi family 1989

One day, Mark came home from school, and I had a feeling that he came in with someone. I asked, "Who is here with you?" He said, "No one." I said, "I know someone is with you." They would tease me and do this all the time. I said, "Okay Matt, where are you? I know you are here." Mark said, "Mom, no one is here. I just have this Ouija board." I told him to get rid of it immediately. I had the strangest feeling someone else was in my kitchen. Mark knew I was serious, because I was very upset. I'm sure he was frightened and in shock to think I could feel something evil around us.

In 1992, my dad passed away after battling heart problems. A short time before, they had moved to the shore, because the taxes were getting to be too expensive at the lake community they were living in. So this meant we had the responsibility. My sister lived in Long Island, and my brother lived in Cape Cod, so my mom wanted to live with me. She thought she would be able to help me with the children. She shared a room with my girls, and then after her house was sold, mom put an addition on our house. It was a beautiful bedroom with skylights, two walk-in closets, and a bathroom with a Jacuzzi tub. It also had a sitting room where she could watch television and get away from the noise and craziness of our house. I really enjoyed her living with us. My mom was the most loving and giving person. She always wanted to serve and help, and she inspired me to do so as well.

I remember when I was a kid in Hoboken. My family and neighbors always helped one another, and I did the same. As kids, we would run to the store for someone or watch their babies in their carriages as they went upstairs to cook. The people across the street owned a pastry shop, and my mom would always help them with their bills since they couldn't read English. They were Italian, and she knew how to read and write Italian very well. Mom was always helping someone, so I did the same. In Hoboken, you could walk to almost anywhere you had to go. That was one good thing about the city. It was much easier to go to stores as they were just around the corner. But here in Florham Park, you had to drive. You'd also see your relatives more often in Hoboken. On Sundays, I would walk down to my other grandmother's house and see all my cousins.

I remember during one Easter holiday, I saw my cousin Linda. Her family had very little, but they always seemed so happy. I wore a beautiful blue taffeta suit that my grandmother made. I remember her telling me how pretty I looked, while she had a little black and white tweed hand-me-down suit on. I felt so bad for her. She was the sweetest person. Now, later in life, we became very close, because something terrible had happened to both our mothers. They became ill with Alzheimer's disease. They were very close growing up.

Her mom became a beautician and was a terrific baker. She won many blue ribbons for her baking. In fact, she made my wedding cake. As our moms got older, Linda lived in Texas, but what brought us together was that both our moms had this terrible disease. We would call each other on the phone on a Sunday night when the rates were lower. Linda and I would talk and laugh about the things they did. We were strength for each other as this was a very hard disease to handle.

Linda's husband left her many years before with four children, so she didn't have to contend with him. However, I had Jim who was not too understanding, which I couldn't believe. He was such a loving man, and he loved my mom. I remember when my dad was not treating my mom right. Jim would get angry about it, so I couldn't understand why he didn't treat my mom with kindness and understanding. He didn't have the patience and just couldn't handle it. He would shout at her for doing something wrong. He couldn't stand her singing or repeating herself. I was devastated to see him treating my wonderful mom like that. I would talk to my cousin and we would pray together. I guess it was because he had so much on his plate with the painting business, running a part-time vending business, me, and all the kids. I guess it was too much for him, so he took it out on mom. I couldn't see him act like this, so I would leave the room, go up to my walk-in closet, kneel down, and pray, "Dear Lord, please take this cup from me. I don't know how much longer I can take this." My mom was the sweetest, kindest person I ever knew, so you can imagine how thrilled I was when she came to live with us.

Some years earlier, before my dad passed, he was not the easiest person to get along with. He was sick and wanted a lot of attention from my mom, and he was very self-centered. He really controlled her. He didn't even like her to talk to us on the phone. So when he died, I thought I was going to give her a much better and happier life. It was good in the beginning, but after a year, when we found out she had Alzheimer's, Jim started acting just like my dad. My mom always did something for someone. She couldn't do enough for you. I can still picture her with a tray in her hands ready to serve someone. When she came to live with me, she said, "I always pictured myself helping you with all the kids." She said this as she folded my laundry. Even with her befuddled mind, she wanted to help. I was truly blessed with a mother like this. I am so proud to say I am a lot like her.

Unfortunately, after she developed Alzheimer's, it had to be the most trying and exhausting time in my life. With mom not remembering anything and singing all the time, teenage boys, two busy little girls, and me working a Mary Kay cosmetics business as a makeup consultant; how I didn't have a nervous breakdown, I'll never know. I do know this, though: God was carrying me through it all. I couldn't have done it on my own. Not without my Lord!

For no reason, Jean started to become very fearful of everything. If she watched something on television that scared her, she was afraid someone was going to climb in her bedroom window, even though her bedroom was on the second floor. We took her to a child psychologist for a while, but it really didn't help. Even though her sister was sleeping in the next bed, she was still afraid. Some nights, I would have to lay down with her until she fell asleep. This was around the same time Jim started getting impatient with Jean, and it worsened as the years went on as he didn't get along with her. It got to a point where she couldn't do anything right. He would put her down, ridicule her, and yell at her constantly. It got so bad that she would come home from school, and as soon as her father came home, she would go up to her bedroom. I can't tell you how this hurt me. I don't know why he treated her this way. Jean was the sweetest girl, and she never gave me any trouble. The more he would get on her, the more I would take her side and defend her. I guess that made it worse for her, and put him and me at odds with each other.

This situation was hurting our marriage. I absolutely hated him for the way he was acting. After some big blow ups, he realized what he was doing to her and apologized. I know he loved her, but he wasn't giving her what she needed: his approval for just being her. I always wanted my children to feel loved and wanted, safe and secure. I couldn't get it across to Jim how he was damaging her. We went for counseling, he would try for a little while, but then it would start all over again. Jean marched to the beat of her own drum, and he couldn't accept it. She was not like him. Jean was forgetful a lot of the time and wasn't too neat with her room, which was nothing like Jim. Gayle, on the other hand, was a lot like him, and this made it worse for Jean. It magnified the problem, although the girls were very close and got along well with each other more times than not. They had their little fights and arguments, but it never lasted long. I hated dinner time, because Jim would be tired and cranky, and would inevitably pick on Jean for something. I always cooked a nice dinner, and it would be spoiled as we all ate with a lump in our throats. The kids couldn't wait to leave the table, and this was not what I wanted for my family.

Being Italian, we always sat around the table long after dinner was finished. We would talk, and laugh, and have fun. This did not happen in my house. The only time it did was if Jim wasn't there. The whole mood of the dinner was different, and everyone was at ease. I didn't want it to be this way, but that's the way it was. I tried everything to change him, but it was no use. Jim was a very moody person who wanted his own way. And on top of it all, he was a perfectionist. Yes, I could honestly say he was very hard to live with. Being in the middle, I always bore the brunt of it.

In Jim's defense, I went to a counselor myself to keep my sanity. I know he had a lot on his plate and took it out on me, Jean, and my mom. He felt he could change her. I don't know what he was thinking. He wouldn't be very nice to mom, which I couldn't bear. So the counselor told me to get out of the kitchen when they were together, and I did just that. I would go upstairs into my walk-in closet, get on my knees, and pray. I wouldn't leave Jim, because I loved him, and I was well aware that he had a lot to deal with. Just think about it. He had a blind wife, a mother-in-law with Alzheimer's, and six kids. Not to mention a painting business and a vending machine business to run. Is it any wonder he acted as he did? Jim was a good provider, and we lived pretty well; and I must admit we didn't want for anything. However, I couldn't stop thinking about what my grandmother used to say, and could never understand what she meant by it until I was going through such a trying time as this. She said, "I feel like I'm spitting blood in a gold bowl." And that's exactly how I felt!

Bea and Jim's 25th Wedding Anniversary

When Jay graduated from high school, he went to County College of Morris. He took computer programming but didn't like it. Jay was more interested in music. Unfortunately, we couldn't send him to a four-year college, because we thought he wouldn't be serious and not study. This was the biggest mistake of my life. I wish I had sent him away, because then he decided to go to The Paperhanging Institute. He liked working with his hands, and made good money doing so. Jay did so well that he gave me and Jim a twenty-fifth wedding anniversary surprise party at The Park Savoy Restaurant. He did it all himself. He sent out the invitations, decorated the room, and even bought dress clothes for the boys and pretty dresses for the girls. I was so proud of him. He even thought of bringing my wedding album there, and played the songs we danced to at our wedding. This was done when he was only nineteen years old, and not even old enough to drink at the bar. I couldn't believe that a young kid at his age would think to do such a wonderful thing for us. Well, I guess we must have done something right!

Bea, Jim, Rae, Peter, Carl and Joyce

All the boys went to County College of Morris for at least a year, then went on to do other things. Glen liked cooking, and he worked at Panevino's Restaurant in East Hanover. So, we sent him to CIA, The Culinary Institute of America. The best culinary school in the northeast. After two years, the day finally came to see him graduate. We sat in a large dining room and ate a wonderful meal cooked by the lower classmen. It was delicious. When the graduates walked in, we stood and applauded. When Glen was to pass by me, he picked me up, spun me around and exclaimed, "We did it! Mom we really did it!" I was so proud of him. I thought my heart was going to burst. With this degree he was able to work at any upscale restaurant. Glen loved to cook with me and was always my right-hand man. It isn't any wonder that we have this special bond. I guess our love of cooking brought us closer. Glen is very dependable and is always there for us and anyone who needs him. Glen is a wonderful person, and the best part is that he loves the Lord. Mark went to county college for a short time, because he didn't know what he wanted to do. Jim had the painting business, and all the boys helped him. Jay still had his own wallcovering business and called it Paperboy. At times, he would work with them on the same job. Steven went to county college too, but he finished, and then went onto Stockton College and received a degree in Criminal Justice. Steven would work with Jim and Jay when he had his days off.

Meanwhile, the girls were in high school and worked too. Gayle was still in dance, and Jean was involved with soccer. She was in varsity for the whole four years of high school. They were very busy girls but still maintained A's and B's, and were always on the honor role. They were very competitive with one another. The girls would have a fit if one got an A and her sister got a B. Nothing like the boys as they were happy to just pass!

As time went on, they all dated. They all fell in and out of love and got their hearts broken, but they went on with their lives until the next one came along. I didn't want to get attached to any girl or guy because within a few weeks, there would be someone else sitting in my kitchen. Glen fell in love in his second year of high school with his girlfriend, Toni. They dated all through college and were married in 1996. Glen was only twenty-four, and Toni was twenty-three. He had a good job at Il Giardino's Italian Restaurant in Cedar Knolls, and Toni worked for an ophthalmologist. The wedding was beautiful. It was so hard for me to think that I was starting to lose my boys, but that's life. I was glad that they were happy. They married at Saint Vincent Martyr—our church in Madison—their reception was at The Brownstone in West Paterson, and they honeymooned in Hawaii. Now mind you, they dated for ten years. So after being married for one year, they separated. I was heartbroken, but after a few months, they got back together again.

The next year didn't start out very well, and little did I know it would get worse. It was so bad that it was totally unimaginable. Our dog, Puffy, had sugar diabetes and had to take shots. The poor thing lost his sight. So when he would walk into a wall, I would tell him, "Come on, Puffy, if I can do it, so can you." From then on, he would walk slowly and no more running around for him. He lasted about six months. One night, while Glen was still living with me during his breakup, he heard him wailing. It was about three in the morning when he woke me up. The sound the poor dog made was awful. We bundled him up and took him to the animal hospital. Unfortunately, he was so sick we had to put him down. It was so sad. Jim and I missed him terribly, and so did the kids. It was like one of the family was missing.

So I kept my promise to myself and my family that when Puffy goes to doggy heaven, I would get a Seeing Eye dog. Well, that didn't go over too well with Jim. I felt this was the best time to go for one as my girls were almost seventeen, and it would be a good time to leave the family for three weeks. I had to live there so I could bond with the dog and get a lot of training, but what I really wanted was a little independence. I needed to get out of the house by myself, and not wait until someone asked me to take a walk or something else I would have liked to do. Jim felt like I didn't need a dog as I had him, my family, and my friends. He just couldn't understand it. He was dead set against it, but I had to do it for myself. After all, I gave everything I had to him and my family, so now it was my turn to think of myself and my future. I had no idea what God had in store for me after my children were all grown-up.

I had just placed my mother in a nursing home a few months before, because she was getting too hard for me to handle. She started to leave the house by herself, and one day, she took a wrong turn. Instead of going around the circle, she went to the right and found herself on Elm Street. Thank God someone saw her and she asked where Murphy Circle was. They told her where to go. She was so frightened. I couldn't take the chance of that happening again. Plus, she was off-balance while walking, and we were afraid she would fall and break her hip. It pained me to place her in Morris View Nursing

Home, but I had no other choice. Especially when I remember the day I had helped getting her dressed, did her hair, and settled her into her recliner chair. Afterward, she took my hand and said to me the words I will never forget. "Bea, I hope someday someone takes care of you the way you've taken care of me." This killed me as this was one of the most difficult decisions I ever had to make, and I will never forget those words.

My brother Carl would take her for me during the summer, but he couldn't any longer. They felt bad because they wanted to help me, but it was getting too hard for them to handle her and work too. My sister couldn't help me either. She would take Mom every January, but her husband was diagnosed with cancer later on. This decision was torturing me, and I missed her so much. I loved taking care of her. I just had to bite the bullet and do it for her safety and my sanity. I know that this would solve a lot of my marriage problems, but it was a very painful time for me. I was really suffering, because I loved her so much, and in my Italian family, you didn't place your elderly loved ones in a nursing home. You cared for them until the Lord called them. It broke my heart, but it was a big help for restoring my marriage. If my mom was in her right mind, she would have told me to put my husband first, and that's just what I had to do. But one day when I was praying, and agonizing over this decision, I heard the Lord say to me very clearly, "Bea, she's not finished working for me yet."

I asked, "Lord, what can she do at the age of eighty?" He repeated it again.

Well, after mom was there for a week, one of the nurses told Jim, "We call your mother-in-law the sunshine lady. She is always smiling and singing. She helps to push people in wheelchairs or gives someone a hug or just holds their hands." Yes, the Lord was right. She still had to do more work for Him. I thought, *At the age of eighty, she is still a servant for her Lord*. I'm sure she touched so many people who had no one to smile or care for them or hold their hand. That was my mom, a servant of the Lord until the very end.

Part 3

A month after Puffy died, I called The Seeing Eye to inquire about how to get a dog. They asked if I walked with a cane and knew my way around. I told them, "Yes, but I want more independence, and I would feel safer with a dog." They also asked how my health was as you needed to be healthy enough to walk at a fast pace. Soon an appointment was made for an interview with me at my house to see if I would qualify for a dog. The next month, a couple of the instructors came to my house to see how well I got around. I showed them how I walked through the area with my cane. Then they had a harness for me to hold onto. One instructor held onto the front of it, while I held onto the handle to give me the feeling of how a dog would pull. They did this to determine if I liked a stronger pull or a lighter one, and at what pace I liked to walk. Then they sized up the type of dog by the pull and by your pace. After the interview, they said I was accepted and that I would be called when they had the right dog for me, and when they had an opening. I didn't want to go in April around Easter time, my birthday, or our anniversary. Also in May was Mother's Day, and I certainly didn't want to be away from my family then. In the summer, the girls would be out of school for their vacation, so I couldn't go then. Well, I prayed really hard for September, because that would be perfect. The only thing I would be missing would be the girls going back to school, and at the age of sixteen, they didn't need me. I knew I'd be missing them getting their driver's licenses, but if I put everything before this, I would never go.

So I prayed in faith that I would be called to go in September. I pictured myself going, and what clothes I would pack. I prayed believing that had to be the right time, and God came through for me. I received a call from The Seeing Eye saying they had a cancellation for September. Delight in the Lord with all your heart, and He will give you your heart's desire.

I always dreamed of getting a Seeing Eye dog, but it was never the right time for one. I did try for a dog after I learned how to get around with my cane when I first lost my sight. But then I finally became pregnant again after my miscarriage, and I wasn't about to have anything hamper my pregnancy as I knew you had to walk pretty fast. I didn't want to lose another baby. At that time, having a baby came first. I did try again when Steven was about to go to school. I called The Seeing Eye and was misinformed. The person told me I couldn't get a dog, because I didn't go out to work. I was so upset and disappointed. It was just as well, though, because that's when I became pregnant with the girls. I had to put it off again, but now was God's perfect timing.

I had never gone against Jim's wishes, but I had to this time. I felt he would come around to my way of thinking eventually. Well, he was hoping he could take me home on the weekends as The Seeing Eye was only a couple of towns away in Morristown. Jim was told he could not do that as I had to bond with the dog and no one else. It had to be me exclusively.

At last, the big day finally came. It was a beautiful Saturday morning. I was so excited! I think I felt like a kid going off to college. After all, I had never been away alone in my life. It was scary but exciting! I was greeted by the administration advisor and introduced to my instructor. Her name was Jane. She showed me to my room, and gave me and Jim a private time to say goodbye. Jim was sad, and I think very angry at me, but it couldn't be helped. I had to do what I had to do. After all, I was the one who was blind, and this time it was about me, not him. I knew it would really hurt the both of us to be apart, because we had never been, except when I had the babies in the hospital; but even then, I saw him every night. Now I would see him only on weekends between the hours of two and four o'clock on Saturdays and Sundays. And anyone else who wanted to come was welcome as well.

It was hard saying goodbye, but we managed. When I was alone, I was a little frightened, but excited. Just think about it. How would you feel being in a strange place, totally blind? Soon, Jane came in and explained to me what would be taking place next and everything I would be doing. I finally heard the words I was waiting so long to hear. I would be getting my dog on Monday. Jane and I went on a tour of the building so that everyone could get acclimated.

The campus was situated on Washington Valley Road, surrounded by mountains and beautiful trees. There were two dining rooms. One was informal, and the other was more formal so that the dogs could get used to being in both types of environments. There was a large lounge where you can entertain your guests that led outside to a quarter-mile path. This was called The Juno Walk where you could practice walking with your dog. It had a few benches along the side of the path, and two gazebos in which to sit. This was on one end of the building. The entrance was in the middle of the building that led into a waiting room with an information desk. The right of the entrance led to a hall with offices on each side. There were separated rugs on the floor. They were placed strategically so you could tell if you were in front of an office or near the entrance of the building. The dorm rooms were in two wings of the main building. One wing was for the women, and the other for men. This was separated by a staircase going up to the second level where there were more dorm rooms and a large comfortable lounge for our meetings. However, every dorm had its own lounge. The steps going down went to the basement where there was the laundry, grooming, and tech rooms. Our dorm rooms were large with tile floors for obvious reasons, one single bed, a mat for the dog, and a small, but ample bathroom. There was a dresser, a desk, and a closet. The headboard of the bed held a radio. Thank God I had a phone, but we couldn't receive calls after nine o'clock, so we wouldn't bother the others. Wow, I was finally here. I couldn't wait until I got my dog.

That evening, I met all the other students and staff. There were twenty students to a class, and we were placed in groups of four. The other students I met were from so many different walks of life. Some were into computers or sales, while others were in different occupations. I was so impressed with how they got along despite their disability.

The next day, Sunday, an instructor drove me and a few others to church. It felt so strange not being with Jim. Well, now I felt like I was on my own. I was a little afraid, but I had to do it. I might have been on my own, but not alone. After all, I had my Lord. The Lord said, "Be not afraid. I go before you. Come follow me, and I will give you rest." I felt very safe. After lunch, we got to meet some of the dogs that would be training for future classes. They were so beautiful, and so smart. This made us all more anxious to get our own dogs. Many people were there for their second, third, or fourth dogs, and so on. The students were expected to dress nicely for meals since they would have tours going through or perhaps business people invited to lunch. But when we walked through Morristown with our dogs, we wore casual clothes and comfortable shoes or sneakers. The meals were delicious, and the staff was wonderful to us.

Meeting her guide dog Becky

On Monday morning, I was called down to the lounge, and there I finally met my first dog. I was so happy, and I felt like crying. Her name was Becky. She was a beautiful German Shepard. I fell in love with her the moment she gave me her paw. She was black with a tan face, and a light tan stomach and legs. Jane was also crying. After all, she was giving me a dog she had trained for about seven months. So it was difficult to give her up, even though she would be training the both of us. When I brought Becky to my room, and tried to get acquainted and start bonding, she wanted to get out and go to Jane. I found it very hard to break her away.

When we started our training in town, it was a little scary; but we had partners, and Jane was right behind us. The instructors never let you go alone. They were always there. We traveled all around Morristown, walking three miles an hour. We had to walk fast so the dog would not get distracted by other animals or something that might look interesting to them. We crossed streets, went in and out of stores and restaurants, into churches, the post office, the courthouse, and many other buildings to get a feel of how to work together. We also rode on buses and trains. Some students had to fly home, so that would be another experience for them. When we crossed a street with a traffic light at the corner, I had to listen for the cars to stop and the cars at the cross street to go. Then we would proceed to walk. But if a car ran a red light, the dog would not go, even if you gave him the command to proceed. Sometimes a car would turn right in front of you, and the dog would stop in the middle of the street. They are absolutely amazing! Of course, you have to give them the commands, and they have to listen to you because now you are their master, and you're a team. Some people think the dogs watch the traffic light change, but that's a misconception. You command, and they lead.

Everyone would go to town twice a day. In the morning for about two hours, and then in the afternoon, after lunch, for another two hours. Now this was after getting up at half past five in the morning, feeding the dog, and then getting them out to do their business. We learned when they eliminated, you placed your foot by their back leg, and put a plastic bag over your hand to pick it up. Then you pulled the bag over your hand with it all inside and threw it away. Yes, we had to do it all. In the evenings, we had meetings, and then we were able to socialize. By nine o'clock you were in bed, and more than happy to be there. Talk about being dead tired!

The first night, Becky cried a lot, but then she calmed down. It was exhausting, but well worth it. When Saturday came, I was so happy to see Jim. I think he was equally as happy to see me. He seemed to like the dog, and said she was very nice looking. The next day, the kids came to visit me, but I think it was more to see Becky. They all fell in love with her, but they couldn't pet her as she had to bond with me. I was glad when Jim told me he had gone to visit my mom at the nursing home one day, and the kids went the other days. I missed her terribly, and couldn't wait to show her the dog.

Bea and Becky on "The Seeing Eye Guide" cover

Well, after three and a half weeks, we were ready to go home, but not after I match-mated a couple I was friends with. Charley was my partner when we walked around town. He would always talk about Donna, another girl in our group. I noticed that whenever he spoke at the table, he would direct his conversations toward her. I knew Donna was going to leave after two weeks, as this was her second or third dog, and she didn't need to stay as long as those of us who were there for the first time, like me and Charley. So the day when she was about to leave as I hugged her goodbye, I told her about Charley and that he was interested in her. I asked if she had noticed, and she said, "No;" but she thought he was really nice. I suggested she leave him her phone number and her email address, so they could possibly keep in touch. Well, they did, but it was hard for them, because he lived in Tennessee, and she lived in Los Angeles, California. Before long, they met again and fell in love. The next September, they were married! I was so happy God used me to help them get together. Many other couples met there as well and were married. You don't need eyes to fall in love; just an open heart!

When I went home, I would have never imagined what life was going to throw at me next. Something so unbelievable, so totally unexpected. Never in my wildest dreams could this be happening. Jane drove me home, but before I went to the house, I asked her to take me to the liquor store. I wanted to give her a bottle of wine in appreciation for all she had done for me. This was my independence day. This could not have happened if it wasn't for her and The Seeing Eye. I also bought wine for Jim, I guess you can say as a peace offering. It was so good to be home, but being away, I felt like I was on vacation not having to make any meals or do any cleaning; but now I was back and mighty happy to be there. I really missed Jim and the kids, and my crazy household. But Jim was not his warm self. I couldn't put my finger on it until later on when I found out why.

Sharing a hug with Becky

Soon after Jane took me home, I finally did what I had been dying to do. I went out alone with Becky on our first walk together. As I walked down the street, I felt so liberated, and so independent that I started to sing, "I'm free. I'm free at last. Praise God, I'm free at last!" This was truly my "Declaration of Independence" day. I felt like a kid that had just gotten their driver's license and was driving alone for the first time. It felt so good to be able to walk by myself. Becky did great, and of course, I was a little nervous, but so elated. When we got back home, I hugged Becky, and cried, "We did it Becky. We did it girl!" I couldn't believe it. With the help of God, I did what I set out to do and reached my goal. I was so proud of myself, and of Becky.

We would walk every day and go a little further every time. One time, as I walked a different way and wanted to cross the street, I tended to lead her. I found myself across the street, but on the other side. I was so embarrassed, because a neighbor saw me and had to walk us back to my house. But that didn't stop me. I just went right back out and let her lead me. The problem was that I wanted her to go straight, but the corner was not directly straight across from the corner I was standing on. So I let her go, and she did it correctly. It was a good lesson for me to learn to never lead her. She leads, and I direct her. It's a fifty-fifty partnership. There were some more mistakes, but we did better as she was getting used to me, and me to her. Also, I had to remember she was young and new to my area. The first year is the hardest, but with a lot of experience, she became a great guide dog.

The next Sunday, after mass, it finally came out what Jim's problem was. We were standing in the back of the church with my daughter Gayle. Someone remarked about Becky and how beautiful she was, and that it looked like she and I would do well together. That's when Jim said, "Now that she has the dog, she doesn't need me any longer. She'll probably divorce me now."

Gayle and I just looked at each other, and exclaimed at the same time, "What?" I couldn't believe he said that. That's what was on his mind the entire time. I have to admit there were a lot of times I contemplated it, and I'm sure he did too. But even though he was a real stinker at times, there was a little thing that held us back. A little thing called love and commitment. When we talked about it, soon after, I proved to him that he will always be Top Dog in my life!

The Bible reads, "My plans are not your plans, and my ways are not your ways." God showed me once again He is truly in control, and something remarkable happened. In the two weeks that I had Becky, she really wasn't bonding with me. Jim and the kids didn't get too close with her, so she wouldn't get attached to them. Well, even though Jim didn't show much attention to her, Becky bonded with him. That dog fell in love with him. She would obey me, but she would follow him everywhere he went. So much for bonding with me! No matter what I did, the instructor and I couldn't change her. He said, after trying to train her and get her away from Jim, "When they love, they love. You can't break it up." Becky would listen to me when we were alone walking, and she would obey me; but she was definitely Jim's dog. At times, it was terrible, because when we went out with her, he had to always be next to me. If he got up to go stand someplace else, she would cry and get very upset. Everyone thought this was so funny, but I certainly did not! No matter what I did, I couldn't control her, and it became very embarrassing. So whenever I went out with Jim, if I could help it, I wouldn't take her with us. What I found so ironic was that Jim didn't want me to get a Seeing Eye dog; yet, she fell in love with him, and Jim felt the same way about her too. God does things in strange ways. God's will is perfect, and this is especially true with what happened next. We both really needed her. Jim and I had to face something awful, and we needed the Lord to get us through this unbelievable time in our lives. It was really bad. Or was it for the better? I'll leave it up to you to decide.

Jim had gone in to see his doctor, because he had pains in his chest and thought he should get himself checked. So they took some tests, and his doctor didn't think anything was wrong, but his assistant just didn't like his color. They did a blood test and said they would get back to him with the results. The day after Jim's fifty-fifth birthday, he received a call from his doctor, and they wanted to see him immediately. My son Mark was home and drove to where Jim was working to tell him. In those days, we didn't have cell phones. Talk about being scared. Boy, we were, as we didn't know what to expect. Well, we walked into the office holding our breath. We sat down at the edge of our seats to hear what he had to say. The doctor said, "Well, Jim, we think you have a blood disease."

I asked, "Leukemia?"

He replied, "You'll have to go to a blood specialist known as a hematologist." The doctor made an appointment with Doctor Wax, a hematologist/oncologist. When we left, we were in shock. We couldn't believe that he had blood cancer. On the way home, I tried to encourage him by telling him we would pray, and that God would get us through this. I prayed for the Lord to give Jim the strength to face what was going to happen, and for me to deal with it all.

When we got home, I immediately called Barbara, as she was a vascular technician and my very best friend. She asked what his white cell count was. I told her 75,000. That's when she said to me, "Bea, that's bad." I died inside. How in God's name was I going to cope with this?

I prayed, "Oh, God, we need your help. Please don't let my husband die!" When we told the kids, they were all in shock like us.

The next day, we got in to see Doctor Wax. He said, "You have chronic myelogenous leukemia. You don't have acute leukemia, which is much worse, and there is no cure for it. We have Interferon, which should help. If it doesn't, well, you'll die. We usually do a bone marrow transplant, but at your age, I feel you are too old." So much for the warm bedside manners.

I thought to myself, *Who does he think he is talking to? This is my husband!* Jim asked him if he minded if we got a second opinion. He told him that we wanted to see Doctor Holland in New York City. He told us to go right ahead since he studied all his books.

After seeing Doctor Wax, we got a call from Jean that she had broken her ankle in a soccer game at school. In our busy household, you always had to expect the unexpected. Jim ran to get her, and took her to the medical group to get it casted. When she got home, she had to get ready and all dressed up, because she was chosen to be one of the princesses for Home Coming Queen at school that night. She asked Glen to escort her down the aisle, but they couldn't get a parking space; so she got out of his car, and walked down alone with her crutches. Jim and I went to see her. We were so happy that her peers nominated her and that she was chosen. Talk about your ups and downs! We sat there with heavy hearts, as we had no idea what our lives were going to be like now.

Doctor Wax immediately started Jim on Interferon. He had to self-inject two shots a day for two weeks, and then Ara-C, another chemotherapy drug, for the next week. Jay would help him with his injections since every other week he was injecting three shots a day. It made him very tired and meant that the boys had to take over the business. Jay was handling the wallpapering, while Mark handled the painting. They both went on the estimates, and Steven helped on his days off from college.

We booked an appointment with Doctor Holland the week of Thanksgiving. Mark drove us to New York City, and we met with him at Mount Sinai Hospital. He tested Jim's blood, and with the chemo they prescribed, it was working. His white blood cells were down to 40,000. So we knew they were on the right track. Doctor Holland conferred with Doctor Wax on Jim's treatment and was very happy with what he had prescribed, saying he would have done the same. Thank God, after a month, his white blood cells were normal at 6,000. But he was no way out of the woods, not by a long shot!

Jim had twenty chromosomes that were bad. Doctor Wax told us we would be lucky if we could cure one a year. But then he didn't know my God and his miraculous powers. I'll explain what I mean. The Sunday after we learned about Jim's disease, a good friend of mine told Sister Dolores—a nun living at Saint Rose of Lima Church in East Hanover—about Jim. When she heard, she came right over with a bottle of holy oil that she had gotten in Massachusetts. At the time, a little girl by the name of Audrey was known to have miraculous oil pouring out of saints in her house. This little girl had fallen in her pool and almost drowned. She lived, but she was brain dead. There was oil coming out of every religious article. Sister had gone up there on a pilgrimage. So when she heard about Jim, she immediately came and anointed him with the oil. I knew beyond a shadow of a doubt that my husband would be healed. I knew from the bottom of my heart, to the depth of my soul, he would be cured. No, it wasn't the oil I believe in; it was my faith in my God! Did it work? Well, you'll just have to read on.

The chemo was working, but Jim was so sick. It was so debilitating, and he was always tired. When he got out of bed in the morning, he would have breakfast and then lay on the couch. He didn't have any energy, and everything was a chore. In that first year, he lost some hair and a lot of weight. It was so hard for me to see him so sick. Jim was always so energetic. Nothing could hold him down, and to see him lying there was difficult and heartbreaking. So to get it all out, since I wouldn't cry or get upset in front of him, I would take a walk around the circle, which was a half mile. I would cry my heart out, and I didn't care if anyone saw me or not. I just had to be alone to pray and talk to my Jesus. I asked him to give me strength through this. I didn't know what was going to happen next or, for that matter, our future. Would Jim die? Could I handle everything alone? Would I be able to raise the children the rest of the way by myself? But then I kept saying over and over again, "I can do all things through Christ who strengthens me" (Philippians 4:13), and I clung to His Word. By the time I returned home, I was ready to face whatever God placed upon me next.

In that first year, ten chromosomes were cured. Already the Lord was proving the doctors wrong! But Jim still had a long way to go. The poor man had sores in his mouth making it hard to swallow, and he lost even more weight. He would get cramps in his legs and it was hard to walk, and even harder to go up steps. I could see he was trying to fight it by driving me to a store, and went grocery shopping once a week. I know he was putting on a brave front for me, but I knew him too well. He was in pain and really hurting. Not only physically, but also mentally. I think there were times he wanted to give up and die, but he didn't want to give up the fight.

During all of this, I know he was getting closer to the Lord. Jim knew who he needed to rely on. I think he realized how bad it was when he couldn't do the bills anymore and didn't care about anything. I mean, he cared about his family and what this was doing to us. He was getting very confused about the business, and Mark was handling everything himself. He was our only means of support. I was so proud of him doing all the work himself. Then, he and Jay took it over completely and handled everything. The estimates, the billing, and the work too. It was a lot for my boys to handle, but they knew that our family depended on them, and we needed the money the work would provide. So we were all in this together. The girls also had after school and weekend jobs. Everyone pulled together. But then again, isn't that what families are supposed to do? We all had to work together and help each other out. So, with this in mind, I also felt I had to do more than I was doing, even though I was taking care of Jim, the house, and the kids. I just felt there was still more I could do financially. The girls would be going to college and that meant more money was needed! I had to help them, as well as myself, if God forbid I would have to face the future alone and without my Jim.

In that first year of Jim's illness, a lot had happened. On February 28, 1999, I lost my mom. It was so heartbreaking to me, because I had just visited the day before I had received the call from the hospital that she had suffered a stroke. I couldn't believe it. When Glen and I went to see her, she didn't seem any different. I walked into her room, and she said to one of the aides, "Oh, there's my Bea." She said, "Hi honey," to my son Glen, as she didn't remember anyone's name but mine. I was happy that she still remembered me at least. As usual, she asked if she could make us anything to eat. She always thought about feeding everyone who came to her house. She had no idea where she was. We talked about the children and Jim, but she didn't know he was so sick. Because even if I had told her, she wouldn't have remembered. We talked about all the recipes she used to cook. My mom was a great cook and baker, and you could taste all the love she would put into everything she made. Then, when I went to the hospital, and she didn't know me or was unable to speak, she just mumbled. It was so upsetting to see her like that. I thought not only could I not see her, but now I wouldn't be able to hear her anymore either. She lasted three days in a coma.

The day she left us, everyone was standing around her bed; my brother and sister, and most of our children. It was such a beautiful passing from one life to another. Rae, Paula, and I sang her favorite songs to her, and we spoke about all the good times we had with her and our children. It seemed to me like she was having a hard time leaving me, as I was her baby girl and she always wanted to take care of me. I told her I would be fine because I was with Jim and my children, and that they would always be there for me. I told her to rest and not be afraid. "Jesus is waiting to take you home." I knew she heard me as a tear fell from her eye that I wiped away. This was her way of letting me know she had heard me. And then she was gone.

My mom died the way she loved to live—with her family all around her. I could not believe she was gone. This person who bore me, raised me, and poured all her love into me and her family, would not be there anymore. I would never feel her arms around me or her kisses. She would hug me so tightly that it was like she wanted to press me right into her heart. I thought I would never hear her voice again until I remembered that I had taped her singing and talking to us on Mother's Day the previous year. I was so happy I did that, but I couldn't listen to it for a very long time. When I did, I just sat and cried my eyes out, because I missed her so much, and I still do to this day. It's very difficult to write about my mom without getting teary-eyed. Going through my past is awfully hard, because all the old feelings come rushing back to the surface. But I must do this as I must leave this legacy to my children, and to let you all know how my wonderful Lord worked in my life. I am no one special, just another child of God. But that's what makes us all so special. After all we are the Kings kids!

My sister and brother let me run the arrangements for her funeral. I did what I thought she would like. I had her looking beautiful for the viewing, and had her hair colored. She looked like she was sixty instead of eighty-two. I think she would have been very pleased. All of the family rose up to say a few words about my wonderful mom. I told everyone there that mom and only the good Lord could live up to the first chapter in Corinthians. It reads, "Love is patient, love is kind, never boastful or proud or envious." At the funeral, all the grandchildren participated in this celebration for my mom's new life with her Father in heaven. I knew that she wouldn't want us to be sad, because she was now getting her rightful reward. When we laid mom to rest at the gravesite, my nephew David said a few prayers since he was a children's pastor in his church in Long Island. We did not linger very long as the weather was bitter and very windy. I think she wanted us to leave and get on with our lives. We had a lovely luncheon, and then everyone was gone.

Now this was the time I was dreading. Being alone with my thoughts, my overwhelming pain, heartbreak, and the futility of it all. There was nothing I could do to bring her back. The only thing I had left of her was my memories. Some were good, and some were hurtful, like all the times Jim was nasty to her when she would repeat herself. He knew she couldn't help it, but it would get on his nerves. He would pick on her for nonsensical things. I couldn't bear it, so we would fight all the time. I felt my father hurt her enough. She didn't need him to hurt her too. So when she died, I knew it was mean and cruel of me to say, but I couldn't help it. I was hurting and angry that my mom was gone, so I took it out on Jim. I know it wasn't fair or right, but I couldn't help myself from saying to him, "Well, are you happy now that she's dead? She can't bother you anymore." He looked at me, just sat down, and cried. I knew he felt a sense of relief not to have this responsibility anymore. I must admit I felt the same when his dad passed away, but it was a bit of a relief not to be a caretaker. You can only do so much, and I felt I did my share. I'm sure Jim felt the same.

I tried very hard to forgive Jim. It was very difficult seeing my mom and daughter verbally abused. He was very cruel to Jean. She would call Glen to come and get her because she couldn't take it anymore. He knew how she felt as he also felt Jim's wrath with the awful things he would say by putting him down mercilessly. So, Glen and Jean became very close. Jim was a perfectionist, but they just couldn't meet his expectations. He really crushed their spirits. I know they will never forget the harsh words, but I hope they can find it in their hearts to forgive him. I know they show him love out of respect for their father. I hope and pray when they marry and have children, they will profit by our mistakes.

We did what we had to do, the best way we knew how. I knew he was sick, but sometimes your own hell is right here on earth, and I know that's what he was going through. I knew he felt guilt, sorrow, and shame. I felt sorry for him, but I know he had to deal with these memories himself and put them behind him. I know God will forgive his harshness to my mom, and for that matter, our daughter Jean. Hopefully, in time, he would forgive himself.

Soon after, I forgave him. I had to, because like the Bible reads, "If you don't forgive, you will not be forgiven" (Matthew 6:15). I knew my mom forgave him the moment after he said hurtful things. She was such a kind, loving, forgiving person. She was an eternal peacemaker. "Blessed are the peacemakers as they are the children of God" (Matthew 5:9). I am so proud when people say I am a lot like my mom. I always want peace and happiness for everyone. She was such a wonderful mother. My mom was a great example of what a true Christian really should be. I am proud to be called her daughter.

Through the rest of that year, Jim continued to visit the doctor every month for blood work. Everything was going well, except he was feeling miserable and very tired. His white cells were down, and his bad chromosomes were gone. He was on the mend, but he didn't think so with the way he was feeling. Although he was tired, we took a vacation up to New Hampshire and used our timeshare. It was about six hours by car, because we didn't want to fly with Jim in his condition. It was beautiful there and very scenic. The house we had was ample, and we swam in Lake Winnipesaukee. I felt right at home as it brought me right back to my childhood swimming in our lake. Becky didn't like me swimming, and she would bark. But when Jim came in, she really had a fit. She'd cry and jump. The kids had a hard time holding her back, although I don't think she would have come in after us. I don't think she liked to swim, and I surely didn't want to find out. We didn't need her jumping on us. So that meant I couldn't swim for very long.

We took boat trips, and saw the Old Man in the Mountain where nature carved out a form of an old man's face. We also rode a lift from one mountain to another. I was so thankful we could do this since it was a nice change to get away from our problems for a week. We all had a good time, except for the girls. At the age of seventeen, they were bored stiff and couldn't wait to get back to their friends. I must admit that at times they made it miserable for me, but I was so thankful we were all together with Jim. We didn't know what the next year would bring.

In the fall of that year, I decided to upgrade my computer skills so that I could obtain a job. My girls would be going to college, and would need me for financial help, and I had to be there for them. So The Commission of the Blind helped me to enroll in The Vocational Center for the Blind in Denville. I went for eight weeks and I had to live there. So I would be driven by Jim on a Monday morning, and one of my children would pick me up on Thursday afternoon. I learned very quickly, as I had a great teacher when I first started selling Mary Kay cosmetics. Her name was Kay Chase, and she was totally blind from birth. I used my computer for all my customers. The little selling I did helped me with re-growing my business; however, it wasn't enough. I needed a lot more money to help my girls. Mary Kay cosmetics sold itself. It is a great product and I have been using it for many years. I would have liked to increase my business, but I was very limited. I was only able to contact people by phone, while other consultants could drive and get around easily. My director, Jo Bruner, was doing very well, and helped me a lot until she was diagnosed with a brain tumor. It was horrible to see her go downhill. I needed to change my course of action for my future. I had to help myself and my family.

Becky and I went to The Vocational Center. It was very nice, and I had a good computer teacher. When I came home on weekends, I had to cook, clean the house, and do laundry. I prepared meals for the week so that Jim and the kids would not have to worry about that as he was so tired all the time; and the girls were busy with school, dance, and soccer practice. Of course, the boys had to work. Every other week, Jim would bring me up on Monday morning, and one of the kids would get me on Tuesday evening. Then someone would drive me back up on Wednesday, and if Jim was up to it, he would get me on Thursday afternoon. This was when he was on two shots a day, which was every other week. In this way, I was home with Jim and caring for him every day as he was even more fatigued. Only God knew how horrible he felt. I prayed a lot and praised God that Jim was still alive to be with me and the children.

The Commission of the Blind sent me to an employment agency. It was called Employment Horizons. This was primarily for handicapped people, and was a very emotional day for me. I was glad to get an interview with them, but upset because my friend Jo had passed away and that day was her funeral. As my Mary Kay director, and very dear friend, I was so happy when she joined our Bible study. She suffered a long time with brain cancer and died a year after her husband, who also had cancer. It was tough for me, because I wanted to say a few words at church. So with that on my mind, it was very difficult to separate my thoughts. Now here I was trying to get on with my new life, while I had to witness laying my friend to rest.

As I walked through the door of Employment Horizon, I had to put my personal feelings aside and face my future. Jim drove me there with Becky. The woman who interviewed me was very nice and put me at ease as I was a little nervous. After all, this was a big difference from being a mom, and housewife. She asked me what kind of work I would like to do. I told her I wanted to work on computers, but also with people. That's when I suggested AAA, the American Automobile Association as it was in my town and I might be able to walk to work. Well, they were looking for someone who would work in customer relations, and they always tried to hire handicapped people. It was exactly what I wanted—working on the computer, and helping people whose cars were disabled on the road. Wow, God never ceases to amaze me! I was at the right place at the right time. The Lord's timing is perfect. The woman told me I had to be tested for the position in Newark where The Commission of the Blind was located. I was very excited, but had to put my excitement aside as I had to say goodbye to my dear friend Jo.

The church was filled with her friends and family. Many people rose to say a few words on her behalf, and so did I. Jo had such faith in the Lord that she would be cured. Well, she was, but not in the way we wanted. She was always optimistic. When it came to doing anything that seemed impossible for her, she would just say in her Southern drawl as Jo was from Tennessee, "I can, I will, and I'm gonna!" The weaker she got, the closer she came to the Lord. She loved Jesus and knew He would help her to the end, and He did. Her faith was quite an inspiration to all of us. The only sad thing was that she didn't get to see her one and only son, Jack, marry a very lovely southern girl. I know Jo would have loved to be there, but then I believe she was there in spirit. Jack and his wife still live in Jo's house. Unfortunately, they don't have any children. Jo would have loved for them to have kids. His wife is a teacher, so I suppose she has all the kids she needs to care for and love.

So the test went well in Newark. The person who tested me was a man by the name of Rick Fox. Soon after I was interviewed at AAA, they hired me in June. I was so happy that I could finally contribute to my family's expenses, but most of all to help Jim. I didn't start working until December of 2000. Everything had to be set up for me, and that took a while as the technicians needed to learn my computer and the software. While I was waiting to start working, I practiced at home. During that year, my daughters Gayle and Jean graduated from high school. Gayle received some small scholarships from various funds, and Jean received a scholarship for Art from the high school. She had to maintain a B average, which she did and even better. They were very hard workers and very conscientious. I was so happy with their great study habits, which was a reflection of their twelve-year education here in Florham Park and at Hanover Park Regional High School.

Gayle was accepted to Rutgers University in New Brunswick, only forty-five minutes away and a great state college. I was so happy she wouldn't be that far away, and could come home on the weekends if she cared to. Jean was accepted to the University of the Arts in Philadelphia, which is two hours away. It is a long distance, but that's what she wanted. When we drove them to their colleges, it was very hard to let them go, especially Jean as she would be so far away. Gayle's dorm room was nice and secure at Douglass' all girl's campus, and I certainly felt good about that.

Now on the other hand, Jean's apartment was situated on the eleventh floor in an old building, in the heart of Philly. It was a total city college, and I wasn't too happy about that. Thankfully, she had a wonderful roommate. Her name was Christina. Her parents were there with her, helping with their apartment. As time went on, we all brought furniture for them. It looked so cute and orderly that after a few months, the girls received an award for neatness and cleanliness. Pretty shocking for Jean whose idea of cleaning her side of her bedroom consisted of shoving everything under the bed. Of course, Gayle's was always neat. When it was time for Jean to dust and vacuum the bedrooms, she did the whole upstairs in ten minutes. So, needless to say, I was really impressed. Wow, what a change! Things were looking good already! Gayle's roommate was very nice, but lacked Gayle's neatnik habits. The girls couldn't have a car the first year, so we didn't get to see them that often. As a result, the phone bills were tremendous, which I would soon be paying with my meager salary as soon as I started work.

I finally started working on December 19, 2000. My first day at work was so exciting for me. This was something I had dreamed of for a long, long time, and it was actually happening. Jim brought me into the call center on Vreeland Road, about three miles from my house. I met with the manager, Gene, and the instructors, Arlene and Paul. Paul was also to be my team leader. I was taught in another room away from the control call center that consisted of about seventy-five people. The people were very nice to me, and they made me feel comfortable. It seemed like a very easygoing office. I took notes on my recorder the first day, and studied everything I was taught that day. The first few weeks, I worked three days a week, then five days a week sometime later. I was earning lower then minimum wage until I was actually working on the job, and this took about three months. As I was learning, I sat in on other call receiver's phone calls so I could hear real calls firsthand.

Bea and Becky working at AAA

When I was finally assigned my own desk, I must admit I was really nervous. The computer was connected to my headset so I could hear the words I typed for the customer's order in one ear, while the phone conversation was piped into my other ear. I'll never forget the first call I received. It was a very disgruntled, older woman. Arlene was also connected to the phone, so she could hear the person and coach me. It was scary, but I did it. Of course, as time went on, I became more relaxed and faster with the calls. I loved what I was doing as I was working at a job I loved, while earning money for my family. This income was primarily for the girl's room and board at college. I never took a penny of it for myself. It all went to them, and I was so glad. The only time I used some money was for birthdays. The girls worked on their summer vacations and during the holidays.

In the year 2001, our son Steven graduated from Stockton College. He had gone to County College of Morris, and then finished at Stockton. His degree was in Criminal Justice. I couldn't believe my sweet, quiet son was going to become an officer of the law. I, as a mother, was very concerned for his safety; but I knew anything Steven put his mind to, he would succeed at. In June that year, he was required to attend The Public Safety Training Academy in Morristown, which he did. He still hadn't been chosen by a police force, so that meant he would have to pay for his education at the academy. I prayed to the Lord, and The Livingston Police hired him. Thank God, they would pay for his education, and gave him a salary as he attended the academy. Not only that, he was also given health insurance.

Now, this meant that Jay would be running the painting business with Jim alone, which he wasn't too happy about. Jay always wanted to get into the music business, but was never given the opportunity as it was a very hard business to get into. He played the piano beautifully. He wrote his own music, and had recorded his own album. I hoped and prayed that something would happen for him in the future, as he is so talented. Unfortunately, he wasn't that aggressive. He didn't like rejection. Then again, who does?

Mark decided to go to school for computer work as a tech adviser. He did well and got a job in Wayne. He was so happy when he graduated, and we were so proud of him. Later on he decided to work for a mortgage company and did very well.

The year 2001 came with quite a surprise, to say the least. Actually, it was more like a shock. A miracle was unfolding. It was when Jim had gone to see his doctor for his usual monthly visit. When he came home, I couldn't believe my ears. Something he was saying was not connecting with my understanding. You know when you win something? You hear it, but you can't comprehend what's being said to you? Did God, whom I love, and knew in my heart, really hear me? Was this answered prayer? Is it possibly true? Did I hear him, right?

Jim came home and was telling me about a miracle drug called Gleevec. This was in pill form, and was helping people with CML. The doctor wanted to put Jim right on it since it was approved by The Food and Drug Administration. He started taking it in June and by September, he had gained back the twenty pounds he had lost. His hair grew back, and the fatigue that he always felt was gone. Praise the Lord! This was what we had prayed for. Hallelujah! I had my husband back! Needless to say, he went back to work immediately and was so happy to do so. He still had to visit the doctor every month and have his bone marrow checked every three months.

Doctor Wax was extremely pleased, because Jim was the first patient to live beyond a few years with CML. With my husband back, and in better health, you can imagine how thankful and happy we were to celebrate the holidays that year. I know in my heart that there is nothing impossible for God. But when it actually happens, it's so unbelievable and so incomprehensible. Through it all, you actually see God's hand in your whole life; the past, the present, and after living through all that, you know he is going to take care of you in the future. Bringing you along every step of the way, He truly means it when He says, "I'll never leave you or forsake you. If I take care of the birds in the air or the lilies of the field, will I not take care of you that much more, my little children?" Yes, what God did for Jim was miraculous, but let's face it. We take for granted everything that he does for us every day, don't we? This miracle pill that Jim had to take was a form of chemo. He probably has to take it for the rest of his life. A small price to pay for getting a new chance at life, wouldn't you say? Now he looked at life through different eyes. He appreciated me, the kids, and the whole world in general. I guess he used to ask himself, "How long do I have left to live to do anything?" But now he could say, "Now I can live to do everything!" He was given a second chance to see and make his dreams come true.

The following year, I was finally appreciated for my efforts at work. Employment Horizons called and explained that I was to be given their first-place achievement award for my work at AAA. The second and third place winners were physically and mentally challenged, but dedicated and hard workers. The awards were given to us at a gala affair held in the ballroom at The Madison Hotel. About 200 people attended, including our congressmen. Of course, the heads of AAA were there, and my family was also invited. Jim and some of my children came, but my girls couldn't make it. It was impossible for them with their obligations at college, and they couldn't make such a trip back and forth in one night; especially Jean coming from Philadelphia.

What a night it was! Can you imagine how awesome I felt to be appreciated for the work that anyone else can do easily? But to do it without sight is another matter, to say the least. When Jim and I arrived, I was greeted by the vice president, Marilyn, and my manager, Gene. The assistant to the vice president, Ellen, was also there. The affair took place in the main ballroom where we enjoyed hors d'oeuvres and a wonderful dinner. At the entrance of the ballroom was a very large poster of me and Becky, and videos of us. Gene had recorded me for a news broadcast on television as a human-interest story about how a blind person can manage in the workforce.

After the second place winners were given their awards and gave their thanks, I was called upon to receive my award. I must admit I was a little nervous, but I did my square breathing to calm myself down, and forged ahead. I felt pretty good about my appearance, as I had just gotten my hair done with blonde highlights in it. I wore a long black dress with my garnet cross next to my heart. So I felt confident that I would do well. I used my cane instead of having Becky since Jim would be with me, and she would be watching out for him. When he's around, she sees no one else but him. When I got up to the microphone, I thanked everyone and said how much I loved my job, the people I worked for, and the people I worked with. I also thanked Employment Horizons for helping me get the job. I told everyone how happy I was to be able to take care of Jim who was fighting Leukemia, and was able to help financially to get my twins through college. I let them know how much this job meant to me. Of course, at the end of my speech, I gave thanks to my Lord and Savior. I quoted Philippians 4:13, "I can do all things through Christ who strengthens me." I got a standing ovation, and was kissed and hugged by my husband and all my family. I can tell I must have touched many people, because I was told everyone had tears in their eyes, even my bosses. Afterward, all of them came up to congratulate me, including Congressman Frelinghuysen. I was able to watch it later, because Jay videotaped the whole speech. I wasn't too nervous about talking in front of so many people, as I had done some public speaking for churches and schools in my town.

The following year, my son Glen's wife, Toni, was pregnant with their first baby and our first grandchild. We were so excited! On December 23, 2002, our little Gabrielle was born. She was beautiful. I couldn't wait to hold her and feel her face. She had a lot of dark hair. When she was first born, they kept her in a little bassinette. When I touched her feet, she started to cry. I told Glen to talk to her as she would recognize his voice, and because he always spoke to Toni's stomach when she was pregnant. Well, he did, and immediately she stopped crying. She knew his voice. What an exciting and happy Christmas that was!

Also that year, Mark got engaged to his girlfriend, Heather. He had met her on the beach a few years prior. I remember him telling me that she was a good girl and very attractive. Of course, it made me think, "Gee, what kind of girls were you going with?" I got to know her pretty well, and I was so happy for him. She was from a different background. Her parents were separated, but she was Catholic and I was glad about that. I could see they loved each other very much, so I was happy for them. When they were engaged, he had asked her at a restaurant overlooking the New York City skyline.

Mark had come home to save some money for the wedding and the move, as he was living in an apartment with his best friend Matt at the time. Six months after, they bought a condo, and he wanted to live there with Heather. Well, I was totally against them living together until they were married. Jim and I didn't approve of that sort of thing, but what my Mark did after showed me how much he loved us, and how much he wanted our approval. What he did spoke volumes about his love and respect for us, and our opinion of him and what he was going to do. He brought me to his psychologist, as he had other problems that I did not ask him about. The woman and I were on the same page. She was Italian and about my age. So she knew where I was coming from. I didn't like it, but what could I do about it? I loved Mark and wanted to make him happy, but I needed him to see my side. After all, I had four more children to face and marry off *the right way*. I couldn't back down on my moral values now, and furthermore, I would never!

So, the best solution I came up with was that we would never go to his house until he was married, and I stuck by that. As my children know, I say what I mean and mean what I say! He just wanted our love and acceptance. I loved him, but didn't like it at all. He lived with Heather, and Jim and I never went to his home. They had many parties with the family, but Jim and I did not go. He saw I meant it.

Mark and Heather were married on November 1, 2003. It was the most beautiful day, and about seventy degrees, which for November was pretty warm. The trees were still wearing their fall colors, and I knew the pictures would be gorgeous. Heather made such a beautiful bride. When Mark saw her coming down the aisle, he started to cry. When she reached him, she wiped away his tears. It was so sweet. Of course, this was all relayed to me by Jim. Yes, these are the times that kill me—being there at your son's wedding and not being able to see him, his beautiful bride, the church, and the flowers. Yes, it truly hurts. These wonderful moments are really hard for me. It really breaks my heart, but thank God, I was able to be there to share in their happiness.

In 2004, the girls graduated from college. Ironically, they were both graduating on the same day. What are the odds of that? They went to different schools and were graduating, not only on the same day, but at the same time. Well, I was very upset, as I wanted to be there for both of them. So I did what I always do when things are not in my control. I took it to the Lord in prayer. I knew He would take care of it for me, and if I was meant to be there for both of them, I'd be there. A month before their graduations, Jean told me that she would be graduating at night, as the speaker couldn't come that morning. This meant we could see Gayle graduate in the morning at Rutgers University in New Brunswick, and then go to The University of the Arts in Philadelphia that night. Is God good or what? He always comes through for me. This is what happens when you totally trust in the Lord.

This next chapter of my life is very difficult for me to write about. After the girls graduated, it was a nice change to have some money to help Jim with our mortgage or anything else we needed. However, this only lasted a couple of years, as the company I worked for was changing. They were competing for higher ratings compared with other offices doing the same work. This meant many jobs would be terminated, and people who remained were given a verbal warning notice. If they didn't comply with what was expected of them in three months, they were given a written warning. If the company felt you were not doing what they asked, you were fired. If you made an effort to change, you were placed on probation for a year. Well, the work environment was awful and a huge change from previous years. The employees had to watch everything they said and did. Everyone was waiting for the axe to fall on them.

Being handicapped, they used another technique with me, as they had to abide by the law. The company tried everything to get me to quit. It all started when my supervisor had her monthly meeting with me. We had a chat like usual, but something was different. She wasn't as pleasant, and she put me on the spot with everything I said. One day, when the vice president was passing by my desk, I asked her, "Where is my new computer? Everyone else is getting a new one."

She said, "You're not getting one." I thought she was kidding, but she wasn't.

One day, my supervisor called me into her office and gave me a calling down. She made a real big deal of a mistake I had made the previous Friday evening. Well, she was starting to get on me for everything. She didn't understand my computer and how it worked, because I had different software. I was sent to meet with Human Resources and my supervisor. She shook her finger at me and told me if I didn't comply, I would get a verbal warning. The next day, when I saw my supervisor, I told her I didn't give up easily since I saw the writing on the wall. They were trying to get rid of me. She said, "Neither do I." I knew right then and there that I had a fight on my hands, and what a fight it was! No person, handicapped or not, should ever have to endure this kind of treatment. I had to meet with my supervisor every week. During these meetings, she ridiculed me, put me down, yelled, and laughed at me. She tried to do everything to make me quit. I took whatever she did or said to me and sucked it up. I felt I could win as I thought I was doing a good job. Besides, I loved what I did.

After the three months were up, I met with her and another supervisor, and was told that they would have to take the next step with me. I signed a paper thinking it was the usual signature process that was done after every meeting. This was done to document that you understood and agreed with the discussion. The next week, I was called to meet with HR. She explained what was expected of me now that I had gotten a written warning notice. I said, "I didn't get a written warning notice."

She said to me, "Well, you signed it."

I said, "I didn't sign anything about a warning notice."

She asked me if they had explained that this was what I was signing. I told her, "No!" Of course, the two supervisors said that they had told me so I didn't have a leg to stand on.

It kept getting worse. They took me off the computer and just had me stuffing envelopes for our members. I always did this between calls, but now I was doing this every day for two weeks. Well, I didn't care as long as I was getting paid. They had a long list I needed to accomplish before I was reinstated by January thirteenth the next year. It was difficult, but I had done everything that was asked of me.

Now I'm making this sound like it didn't affect me. But by this time, after all the abuse I was taking, I couldn't sleep, I lost weight, and was losing my hair. That's how upset I was. Every day, Jim would pick me up from work, and he would tell me to quit. I would tell him the same thing every day, "Quitters never win and winners never quit;" and I meant it! It was hard to do, but I did it. It hurt Jim to see me going through this ridicule every day, and seeing me come out crying and so upset.

After I felt I had accomplished everything they wanted of me, they still weren't satisfied. I was supposed to be placed on probation, but my supervisor wanted to have me observed for another month. Yes, they were really putting me through the wringer. One week they would tell me to do one thing, then the next week it was the opposite. I didn't know if I was coming or going. I only knew that they were trying to wear me down, but I hung in there! After a while, they alienated me from everyone else. I was alone in my pod that consisted of six cubicles. I was the only one there, so I'd be unable to talk to anyone or ask any questions. I asked my supervisor, what if I needed a question answered from a member? She said, "Well, use your own discretion." Oh sure, if I ever said the wrong thing, I would be called out on it. She didn't want me to call her on the phone or ask any questions or ask any other team leaders. So I didn't call her on the phone. I would instant message her. Of course, she didn't want this either. Are you getting the picture? Gee, do you think they wanted me to quit? Of course, and they did this so I couldn't collect unemployment.

This company didn't know who they were dealing with. I was going to fight them every step of the way. One day I spoke to human resources, and I asked her, "Why are they doing this and trying to get rid of me?"

She said, "We are doing everything by law, and I should do everything my supervisor tells me to do." Then she had the gall to tell me that she would pray for me. Yeah, thanks a lot! I think she was praying for me to quit so she wouldn't have to go through the problem of firing me.

After I heard they were doing everything by law, I got right into action. I was able to retain an excellent corporate lawyer. As time went on, I was given another supervisor who I really liked and admired. He tried to help me as much as he could, but he was corporate. In the last few weeks I was there, we met every week and I thought I was going to be able to stay. Unfortunately, during the last two weeks, we hadn't met. So when I did see him, I would ask him how I was doing, because he knew how much I wanted to hold onto my job. He would tell me I was doing fine and just to keep doing what I was doing. So I thought maybe there was still a chance.

On the second of May, there was a mistake made by the night supervisor, and I didn't want to get blamed for it. So I went to the manager and told him about the problem, and that the mistake wasn't done by me. I told him I wanted to do everything right, because I wanted to keep my job. He said very sadly, "Yes, I know."

When I walked out of his office, I said to myself, "Yeah, but you're still going to fire me anyway."

On May third, I had gone to Bible study. When I got home—this was Wednesday, my day off—I received a voice mail from HR on my answering machine. I didn't know why they called me. I thought, *Could they be calling to fire me over the phone? No, they wouldn't do that over the phone. Or would they?* Well, guess what? That's exactly what they did. When I called them back, the HR representative said they had to terminate my position as I had made four mistakes that month, and I had to go. I was in good self-control since our Bible study that day was focused on that very topic.

I politely told her that this was discrimination. Of course, she argued with me and said it wasn't, but I could tell she didn't like hearing me say that. She said they would give me good references, and being that she was on the board of Employment Horizons who helped me get the job, she would put in a good word for me. I asked her, "If I'm so good, why are you getting rid of me?" She ignored my question and told me that my desk would be cleaned out, and everything would be sent to me. They obviously didn't want me near the place.

I was in shock, to say the least; I was numb. I felt like I was in a fog, and I just couldn't believe that they would actually fire me over the phone. When I asked her about that, she only replied, "Oh well, you know with Becky and all." The truth is that they couldn't bring themselves to look me in the face, which left me with bottled up anxiety. I didn't get a chance to tell them what I thought of them and how poorly they handled things. I'm sure it wouldn't have done anything to change their minds, but at least I would have gotten it off my chest.

After receiving this call, I was alone. So I put the harness on Becky and went out for a walk. My son Steven was mowing the lawn, and I remember him saying to be careful so I wouldn't trip on the hose that was across the walk. I didn't reply, because I was in a state of shock. Becky and I just walked and walked. I guess when she got too tired, she took me home. I can't tell you how upset I was; so much so that I couldn't even cry. When I arrived home, Jim and Jay were there for lunch. I walked in, and Jim asked me, "What's the matter with you?" I just looked at him, shook my head, and said nothing. While I was going upstairs to our room, he said, "It looks like something's wrong with you." I ignored him, and just went into my room and closed the door. I sat on my bed and just stared ahead. I just couldn't believe it. After trying so hard, they let me go anyway.

Soon after, Jim came up into our room, and demanded, "Something is bothering you, so tell me what it is."

I looked at him and said, "I was fired today."

He asked, "How? Over the phone? Those SOB's." He couldn't believe they could be that cruel to fire someone over the phone. He took me in his arms and cried the tears I couldn't shed. After that, Jay called all his brothers and sisters. The boys were at our house within the hour, cursing them, and sympathizing with me. My daughter Jean called and was crying over the phone as she wanted to be with me; but she was at work and couldn't leave. Gayle called from her job and was so upset for me too. She did something I will never forget. She sent me daisies, the flowers I love, with a card saying exactly what I always said to lift them up. It said, "Remember, Mom, your disappointment is God's appointment for you to do something else. Enjoy your free time!"

The next day, I called HR and asked if they tried to get updated software for me. She said, "Yes, but we spent too much money on you already, and we can't spend anymore."

So I said, "Is that why I was let go?" She didn't answer me. She said she had to go since she was busy. When they started getting new computers, they called The Commission of the Blind. They were told that it would cost about 2000 dollars. Well, they weren't going to pay that, but then I called after I was terminated and learned it just needed to be updated with the software I already had. It would have cost them about 400 dollars, and if I had told The Commission of the Blind that they didn't want to pay for it, I'm sure they would have gotten it for nothing. So that's exactly what I got fired for—nothing!

I sued them for discrimination. They did not give me a new computer like everyone else. I was shut off from everyone and was denied necessary implements for my computer to do my job. They were served notice of the suit and wanted to settle out of court by giving only a small monetary compensation that I immediately refused. I heard later that the Vice President was fired in November. I admit I was pretty happy, because she was the one calling all the shots. It took three years, but I was finally compensated with a lot more money. We settled out of court, and I know I could have received more if I took it to court. However, that could have taken another three years, and perhaps I would have come out with nothing. With all their documentation, I only had my story, which was the God's honest truth; but the judge could have possibly thrown it out and I would have gotten nothing. So, all in all, I did pretty well, and I wasn't greedy. I was gratified to realize not only did they pay me, but they had to pay their lawyers a good chunk of change too. "Vengeance is mine," said the Lord, "I shall repay" (Romans 12:19), and He surely did!

This company really used me for all I was worth. They made it look like they were out to help the handicapped, but in truth they were out for themselves. My picture was taken with Becky often, and it was shown in their monthly magazine and on their website. I also gave them free publicity when I did inspirational talks at the churches and schools. I appeared in a video for The United Way, and of course said I worked for this company. So it looked like they were so wonderful!

It took a long time for me to get over the pain. A really long time. I should say years! It's only now that I can write about it, and not get angry and sob. But I can honestly say I am over it now. I have forgiven them, because as I have said many times before, "If I don't forgive, I will not be forgiven." God has taken care of me through all of this, and I know he will take me the rest of the way right along with Him!

So here I was, out of a job. The first thing I did was get in touch with Employment Horizons, and they immediately gave me an interview. I had to brush up on my typing skills and speed, which I did. One of the counselors brought me to a few companies for interviews. I am very proud to say that when I was tested, I scored an A. I was also asked by Employment Horizons to do a video for them. I was to explain that I was looking for another job since my previous job was terminated due to outsourcing. Actually, this was true, because the company was sending out work, and they wanted to lay off many people, including me. I happily did the video for them, because they were very good to me. I just found out recently that I am still featured on their website seen typing at my computer.

I felt like a fish out of water by not working. I tried getting a job, but they were all quite far away. Jim would have to drive me both ways, which could be an hour to and from home, and I couldn't let him do that. Reluctantly, after about six months of trying, I gave myself permission to retire, despite wanting to do something besides housework and cooking. To get myself away from the house, I joined The Senior Citizen's Club and AARP. Also, I was now free to go to my beloved Bible group on Tuesday mornings, instead of Wednesdays, which was changed to accommodate my day off.

When I was still working in 2003, Jean met a wonderful young man. His name is Domenick. She met him on a social media site. When he saw her name, he asked her if she knew Mark Guzzi, and she told him that he was her brother. She then found out that they went to high school together, and that Domenick was six years older than she was. Jean then asked her brother about him, and Mark said that he was a great guy, but he wasn't too happy about one of his little sisters going out with a much older guy. They spoke online for quite a while, and then she couldn't stand it anymore and had to meet him.

One weekend, when she came home from college, she and her girlfriend Caitlin drove to his house since he lived in East Hanover, only a town away. He worked at his father's pizzeria right in Florham Park. She had gone there so many times and never met him. Well, the rest is history. They took one look at each other, and that was it;

love at first sight! He's tall, very muscular and good looking, and she is a beautiful girl. Needless to say, the next year they became engaged.

Jean's engagement was so romantic. Our family was going down to the shore to Long Beach Island where my friend, Marie, gave us her mini mansion to use for a long weekend. Dom had asked for our blessing just before we left, and of course we said, "Yes;" and we were so happy. The next day, Dom told Jean he wanted to practice his guitar playing and singing, because he was going to perform for us after dinner. They went upstairs to the lookout point on the roof.

As the sun was setting on the bay behind her, and Dom was singing, Jean was sitting there listening to him and looking at the majestic ocean with its rushing waves hitting the shore. Little did she know what was about to happen. Dom said, "I'm going to play the first song we both loved, but now this is a new first for us." He then got on his knee, presented her with a beautiful diamond ring, and asked her to marry him.

Her reply was, "Yes!"

They kissed, and he held her in his strong arms. When they came down, we had the champagne ready to pop, and no one knew but Jim and myself. Dom came to me, before they went upstairs, and told me that he was going to ask her then. Well, my daughter Gayle heard him and guessed it. We all went out on the lower deck to hear him sing, but that's all we heard until they came down. We were all so happy and excited for them. Domenick's parents gave them a beautiful engagement party. They decided to wait a year and a half to save money for their wedding, and she was still a little young at only twenty-three.

In October of the same year, 2005, Steven and Dominica were also engaged. They drove up to Vermont to see the changing of the autumn leaves. Unfortunately, it was raining, so he made it very romantic by strewing rose petals throughout their room, with lighted candles and romantic music. When she walked in, he sat her down and asked her the question she had been waiting for quite a long time to hear. It finally happened, and they were married on September 29, 2006 in Holy Family Church on a beautiful, sunny day. Dominica was glowing, looked so lovely, and her gown was just beautiful. Their reception was held at The Chanticler in Millburn, and they honey-mooned in Aruba.

I was very happy for Steven, but I was losing my baby boy. All of the boys would help out if we asked, but the only one who did everything for Jim and I was Steven. We never had to ask him, he just did it. So when the wedding was drawing closer, I was becoming very depressed. He was so dependable, always there for us, and Jim and I have a very close relationship with him. It was very tough letting him go.

The day before his wedding as I was praying in my kitchen, I was crying so hard and loud in the early hours of the morning that my son Jay heard me and thought someone had died. I couldn't help myself. My heart was breaking, because I knew it would never be the same for us. I was happy that he was marrying a wonderful girl that he truly loved, and they would be very happy. I also know that when you marry off your daughter, she is your daughter all through life. But your son is your son until he takes a wife, then you lose your son. I knew this fact very well from my other two sons who were married. It was very hard to adjust to, but you get used to it. It just takes a little time.

Also that year, on March 28, 2006, my grandson, Michael, was born to Glen and Toni. This made up for marrying off your children. Grandchildren are the best. They bring so much love to a family. I love and enjoy them so very much. They were the bright spot in my life that year while going through the loss of my job. Trying to help the kids with their weddings was another reason why I needed to work, but God helped us find a way to help them. When you rely on God's promises, He is always there for you.

Steven and Dominica also set their residence in Denville in a lovely townhouse. Dominica is a speech pathologist for handicapped children, and Steven is a police officer and works the night shift. I don't get to see them that often. I'm so happy they all live only twenty minutes away. I get to see Jay and Mark a lot as Jay works with Jim, and Mark is in sales. Glen left being a chef to be with his family more. The hours took him away from them for too long. He was asked to work as a title insurance salesman for the same company his wife Toni worked for. Since he is always on the road, he stops in a lot too.

Domenick and Jean were married on April 29, 2007, at Holy Family Church in town, and had a wonderful reception at The Valley Regency in Clifton. Jean wore the most exquisite gown made by Vera Wang, and she was absolutely gorgeous! Yup, another killer day for me, but I got through it. I wore a lovely yellow-gold gown, and trained myself not to cry. Not only did I not want to ruin my makeup, but I wanted to look happy for her on her day. I knew I could cry the next day in the privacy of my own home, and boy did I. It's hard for a mom to let her little girl go, but I knew she was very happy; and Jim and I loved Dom. We knew he would take good care of her, love her forever, and that's all we wanted for her. Dom and Jean honeymooned in Aruba, and the newlyweds moved into their little love nest. It was a cute house in Denville, the town where her two brothers lived.

Bea and her friends at Jean and Domenick's wedding

The same year Jean was married, Jay bought a condominium in Morristown, and I only had Gayle living at home; but I knew before long, she would be leaving too. At the time, Steven was still in the Police Academy, and a fellow student named Patrick Cooper caught wind of Steven having younger twin sisters. One was married, and one was single. Pat bothered Steven everyday about his single sister, Gayle. He never saw a picture of her and knew nothing about her. Steven became frustrated with Pat's antics, so he mentioned him to Gayle and showed her a picture of him. She thought he was a good-looking guy. Many months later, they finally met at a bar in Morristown. Pat said about two words to Gayle, and she turned to her best friend Caitlin and said, "Great, another quiet one!" But he ended up being the opposite! They talked for 2 hours at the bar that night, and Caitlin said to Gayle, "Gayle, you are going to marry him!" Gayle and Pat dated for three years, and he wanted to save money for a ring and a house. He was a police officer in West Caldwell, and she worked for The Chronic Liver Foundation as an event planner and did a lot of traveling. They were engaged in January 2009, and it went like this:

On their third anniversary, he had taken her out to dinner at a very expensive restaurant, and she thought he was going to pop the question but he didn't. The next day, as she was getting ready to go ice skating with him in New York City, she was complaining to me and questioning when he was going to ask her. I was laughing behind the door as she was ranting and raving about how she was going to be eighty years old before he decided to propose.

Pat had actually asked us for our blessing the previous Saturday morning. Jim and I were still in bed when he rang the doorbell. Jim answered the door, and came back up with joy in his voice. I pictured a big smile on his face as he said, "I think he's going to ask us for our blessing!" I quickly got up, put on my robe, brushed my hair, and ran downstairs.

I must say he seemed pretty calm as we sat down, and he began by asking, "Well, you know how Gayle and I have been dating for a while now?"

I answered, "Yes."

He continued, "Well, I'd like to marry her and have your blessing."

Jim and I jumped up, hugged him, and said, "You've got it!" He then told us where, when, and how he was going to ask her. He was planning to take her ice-skating at Bryant Park in New York City, and he wanted to have both families and all their friends over when they returned home.

As it turned out, it was better than he had planned. There were too many people skating at Bryant Park, so they decided to go on a Hansen horse and carriage ride through Central Park. As they were riding, he asked her, "Gayle, what kind of ring do you want?" As she was looking out of the carriage, she told him the style she would like to have. Then he asked, "Is this the one you wanted?" She turned to him, and he asked her to marry him.

Of course, she said, "Yes!" Pat couldn't get on his knee, but she was very happy anyway. The driver asked what was going on. They told him and he took a picture of them with their camera. They went for a drink and enjoyed the special moment in their lives. On their way home, they called all of us and we were waiting for them with hugs, kisses, and champagne. They were happy and so in love!

Gayle and Pat set the date for March 13, 2010. They bought a house in Denville near her brothers and sister, and lived home while they fixed all that needed to be done in the new house. This helped them save more money for the wedding, along with our and Pat's family's help. In this part of the country, weddings are extremely expensive.

When their wedding day finally rolled around, it was not a pretty day. It had to be the worst day of the year as we had a nor'easter rainstorm. Gayle had to make a run for it to the car as it was coming down in sheets. Earlier, she asked me, "Hey, Mom, I thought you prayed for a sunny day?"

I said, "I did, but God said no." When she walked down the aisle to Pat, she was the happiest bride, and the most beautiful. She looked like she was bursting out of a flower in her gorgeous gown. I wore a purple gown this time. This day had to be the hardest of all the weddings for me to get through. After all, she was the last one to leave our home, and Jim and I would be in an empty house again.

We had to go back to where we started. But that's the circle of life, isn't it?

They were married in Madison at Saint Vincent Martyr, the church the girls attended until they were teens, before going back to Holy Family Church here in Florham Park to be with their friends. The reception was held in West Paterson at the Westmount Country Club. Gayle was an event planner at her job, so you can only imagine all the preparation and effort she made for her wedding venue. It was truly remarkable! The things she did and thought of were so outstanding. Gayle certainly had everything just the way she wanted it to be, and she went all out. The food, music, and atmosphere were outstanding! But, then again, I didn't expect anything less, knowing her ability and vast experience in event planning. Gayle and Pat honeymooned, but not in Aruba. She had to be different, and they went to Saint Kitts Island. Upon their return, they moved into their beautifully finished home. It had to be absolutely perfect to meet Gayle and Pat's requirements!

Unfortunately, while everyone was getting married and moving on, Jim and I were told by Glen and Toni that they were going to separate. They were having problems for many years, but I had hoped and prayed for them to make the best of whatever was happening in their marriage. They tried, but it was no use. I hoped they would miss each other by not living together, and that they might get back together, but that didn't happen. I knew their kids would suffer the most, and I didn't want that for my grandchildren. It broke my heart to know they would be raised in a broken family. It's not a marriage staying together just for the kids. Glen and Toni didn't love and cherish each other as they once did. Unfortunately, when that happens, and there isn't any more respect for each other, it's over and done! My heart broke for them and the children as Toni moved out into a rented townhouse. Glen stayed in their home so there would be a sense of consistency for the children. It was really hard for all of us to adjust; but with the love we had for both of them and the children, we all got through it.

That May, my Seeing Eye dog, Becky, died at twelve years old from cancer. Being I had a dog for ten years, I needed to get another one. So, in September I went back to The Seeing Eye and trained with another beautiful Shepard. She and I bonded quickly. Her name was Beth, and she only had eyes for me. She worked with me very well, was very affectionate, and loved to play. When my grandkids played in my backyard, she wanted to play ball with them. I had to hold her back as she would puncture the balls with her sharp teeth. Unfortunately, she also died from cancer in 2018 at the age of ten. I miss her terribly.

In that same year, on July 7, we were blessed with another granddaughter, Lianna. She was Mark and Heather's first, and was so beautiful! The next year, on July 1, 2010, another beautiful blessing was given to us. Steven and Dominica's little baby girl, Gianna, was born. I kept praising the Lord for all these wonderful blessings. Too bad my bubble of euphoria was burst after being with my new baby girl. Glen walked Jim and I out of the hospital and announced that he was divorced. If you want to know how to get on a high and then be dropped back down to earth, that was it. I felt such a loss and hopelessness as I knew they would never get back together. I still prayed and hoped a miracle would happen, but it wasn't meant to be. It was their life, and as much as I didn't want to accept it, I had no other choice. I always felt that marriage was for better, for worse, and for keeps! I guess for them, it wasn't. I just wanted their happiness, and who was I to stand in their way? Our family will always stay close with Toni. I will always feel that she is still part of our lives, and she will be included in everything. After all, she is my grandchildren's mother. I thank God it wasn't a nasty divorce. They both get along for the children's sake. Gabrielle and Michael get a lot of love between the two families, and I think they feel and know it.

Bible group Christmas party

The beginning of 2011 was pretty traumatic for me. On January first, we were having our annual Christmas party at my house. Everyone was too busy, so we had to have this year's party after Christmas day. That morning, as I was taking my shower, I found a lump on my chest the size of a golf ball. I asked, "What is this?" Jim was shaving at the same time, and I showed it to him. By the sound of his voice, he was in shock. When everyone came over, I asked my friend Connie, who was a nurse, what she thought of it, but she couldn't really say.

The next day, I called my doctor and he saw me immediately. He sent me for an X-ray, and then sent me to a surgeon. He checked me over, and then I was sent for an MRI. He called me later that afternoon and gave me the news. I had a tumor under my muscle. It was about one and one-half inches in size and was pushing up on the muscle. I asked him if it was cancerous, and he answered, "Oh, yes!"

I was in my bedroom at the time, so I ran downstairs to get a pen to write the name and number of the orthopedic surgeon at Mount Sinai Hospital in New York City. Jim took one look at me, and asked me what was wrong. I simply said, "It's bad." He became so upset that he couldn't think straight. I told him to talk to the doctor who was waiting to tell him the information over the phone. He was so nervous, he couldn't comprehend what the doctor was saying. I had to be calm for both our sakes.

The following day, I made an appointment with Doctor Wittig who was the top surgeon, and with Doctor Holland who was Jim's doctor whom he had conferred with about his leukemia. My daughter Gayle and my son Mark came with us. They wanted to ask the doctors questions that perhaps we would not think of asking or to help retain what we may have forgotten the doctors telling us due to being so nervous. Doctor Wittig told us that he would have to do a biopsy to see if it was malignant, and I would have to stay in the hospital two days after it was surgically removed. We told him we were getting another opinion from Dr. Holland. He said, "Go right ahead. He is the godfather of this hospital."

Doctor Holland was a renowned doctor at Mount Sinai. They even named one of the new sections of the hospital after him. Doctor Holland is eighty-six years old and is still practicing medicine. He does a lot of cancer research, especially with leukemia. If it wasn't for him and Doctor Wax, Jim wouldn't be here today. So it wasn't any wonder that we definitely wanted to get his opinion. Well, when I saw Doctor Holland, he gave me a physical like I'd never had before. He didn't want to leave any stone unturned. I told him I was going to get a CT scan in a few days as ordered by Doctor Wittig. He said, "No you are not. You are going right now as I have a little pull here!" I had a CT scan and a bone X-ray. The next week during my visit, he informed me that I had myeloma. It wasn't multiple myeloma, because it hadn't gone into my bones yet.

The following week, I went back to New York for the biopsy. The surgery was set for nine o'clock that morning. This meant we had to leave very early. My son Glen drove us into the city on the worst day of winter. We left at five o'clock, as it was snowing and sleeting. The roads and visibility were so bad, I don't know how he got us there. Luckily, as we got closer to the city, it was raining more than sleet or snow; and being that it was so early in the morning, all the traffic lights were set to green. So we made it right on time. Not only was I nervous about the surgery, we had to deal with the weather too! While praying for us to get there safely, I also prayed for the tumor to pop out without having to go for another surgery and having to stay at the hospital for a couple of days. I know Jim hated the city and would not appreciate going back, and forth; but knowing him, he would stay with me the whole time.

Ask and you shall receive the Bible reads. When I came out of surgery, Jim told me as the doctor went to snip a piece of the tissue, the whole tumor came out in his hand. Now how marvelous is our Lord? I was very happy it was out, but unfortunately it was malignant. I had to undergo six bouts of chemotherapy. Thankfully, I went to Mount Sinai Hospital for the first treatment. Then I had the remaining treatments at Summit Medical Group under Doctor Wax's care, while keeping Doctor Holland informed of my progress.

In July, I went into remission. Thank God for these wonderful doctors, and the love and support of my husband and children, because they were very shaken up by this. Especially because they went through this with their dad, and now me. I was very touched by the love and concern they had shown me through that awful time in my life. I truly felt the love from all of them with their reactions after hearing it was cancer.

I'll never forget how my son Glen broke down on the phone while telling him about the cancer. He asked, "Why you, after all you've been through, Mom?" It broke my heart to see my husband and children watching me going through this. To tell you the truth, I felt sorrier for them than myself with all I had to face. But you know what? We got through it. I had to be tough and strong for them. With their love, and my faith in my Lord, He gave me the strength to go on!

Although the chemo had healed me, it compromised my immune system. I was diagnosed with rheumatoid arthritis and was prescribed medications that caused chest pains and landed me in the hospital. Shortly after, I was rushed in again due to severe pains in my arm that turned out to be arthritis, inflamed nerves, and carpal tunnel syndrome.

In October that year, I was rushed to the hospital again, but this time for atrial fibrillation of the heart. This was a day when we had a freak snowstorm on Halloween. It was snowing so hard that the trees were breaking from the excessive weight of snow and autumn leaves that still remained on the branches. It was a mess all around. There was no electricity, and I upset myself worrying about my children. I was very concerned about Gayle being home alone as they called all the cops in, and Pat had to go to work. I was discharged after I was told I had a low thyroid, and was placed on medication for it. After seeing a pulmonary specialist, I was given heart medication. So now I found myself on all these different medications, never having to take any in my life before. What a change that tumor and chemo made in my life; but thank God I can still talk about it, and keep feeling well due to my medications.

That year something wonderful happened. My daughter Jean gave birth to a beautiful baby boy. On December 13, she gave birth to our Nicholas Logan. He weighed nine pounds, and nine ounces. Wow! The poor girl was in labor for twenty-seven hours before they performed a caesarean section that she was very upset about. That year started out pretty lousy, but it ended up being wonderful with our new baby boy; and the announcement from Gayle that she and Pat would be expecting their baby next July was a bonus! Yes! We are blessed. Very blessed indeed!

On July 2, 2011, Gayle and Pat had a little girl. Another beautiful and chubby baby. Her name is Madison Brielle. She weighed eight pounds, and three ounces. Unfortunately, Gayle had a tough time too. She started having labor the day before, but it stopped. She had gone to the hospital and they sent her home. When she went again, the doctor was going to send her home again as she was only one centimeter dilated. She refused to go and just walked the halls. After a long while, she dilated two centimeters and they finally admitted her. The labor was long, and then our precious baby was born. Pat took forever to come out and tell us what they had. They didn't want to know beforehand, as they both wanted the thrill of finding out at the time of delivery. They felt it was more exciting that way, and I agree.

Well, now I'm up to 2012. The Lord has truly blessed us with our six children and beautiful grandchildren. Of course, we must take the good with the bad, as is the case with everyone's life. At the beginning of this year, Jim and Jay disbanded the business, because they both needed spinal surgery. Jim's sciatic nerve was being compressed by a herniated disc and causing nerve pain down his leg. It took a little time, but within a few months after surgery, he was relieved. Jay, on the other hand, had four bulging discs, but one severely herniated and also caused severe nerve pain down his leg. Thankfully, he had some relief immediately after surgery. The unfortunate problem was it left him with severe back pain. Their surgeries were a week apart and they had outpatient surgery, which was great since they both didn't have to stay in the hospital overnight. We hoped Jay's pain would subside, but it didn't.

As you can imagine, we were really hurting financially. Jim and I lived on social security and some investments, but Jay was disabled due to his back condition and can't work. Luckily, his wonderful girlfriend, Andrea, had been helping him; and with the two of us, he was getting by. He didn't have disability insurance, and the government refused him Social Security Disability. He was really upset with his situation, hired an attorney, and appealed their decision. Jay was still writing his piano music, and with the help of God, his music will be appreciated someday. He had an appointment in New York City to see one of the top surgeons in the country. I hoped and prayed he could get him some relief from the pain.

Well, the results weren't too encouraging. The doctor ordered a CT scan and it showed a fractured vertebra. Just great! As if he didn't have enough problems! Now they're recommending another surgery, a spinal fusion that is a more serious surgery and has a much longer recovery time. Also, this doctor can't perform the procedure, as he doesn't participate with Jay's insurance. This is very upsetting, and he has some difficult decisions to make. This poor guy can't win! He plans to go back to the surgeon that performed his last surgery, because they're ordering a SPECT bone scan to evaluate his spine and its ability to successfully fuse if he pursues the spinal fusion surgery.

On the happier side of my life, Jim and I were able to go on vacation with our timeshare to Marco Island in Florida. We needed to get away and recharge. We had a wonderful time just being together alone. Our house is like a swinging door, which I love, and the boys are always coming over during the day. Jay lives close by, and Glen and Mark are in sales so they drop in whenever they're in the area. Steven being a cop, I don't get to see him too often, except when he is watching his daughter Gianna, and he comes over to help Jim with our yard work. He's great like that and I get to have my Gianna all to myself. She is two years old and a lot of fun. She's saying everything now and rightfully so. After all, her mother is a speech pathologist. I don't get to see Mark's daughter, Lianna, all that much as she is in day care all week. She is three years old already. Dear Lord, where does the time go?

The year 2013 was not a lucky year for me. Unfortunately, I was diagnosed with multiple myeloma, cancer of the bone marrow. Two years prior, I had the tumor removed and went through chemotherapy treatment. Now it's come back and in a big way. I was diagnosed in March and went under a lot of chemo. The pain was excruciating and I couldn't take any pain pills, because they made me so sick. I had such pain in my ribs and it killed me to move, especially in bed. Jim had to turn me over from side to side, and lift me out of bed in the morning, because the pain was so awful. He had to help me get dressed, and took care of my every need all day long. My kids were there to help when they could. Jay and Andrea were always over since they lived closest to us. I was in such pain, that a number of times, I told Jim to leave me alone and let me die. I didn't think I was going to make it. But Jim kept encouraging me. He knew what he was talking about after going through leukemia.

Bea during chemo treatment

After all the chemo treatment, I was in remission, but I still had to undergo a stem cell transplant. They remove all your white cells, red cells, and platelets. They harvest them, which removes all the cancer, and then replace them back into your body within a week. My immune system was no longer there, and I had to stay in the hospital for two weeks to build it back up again. As a precautionary measure, everyone who came to visit me had to wear masks, for if I caught any germs, it would be fatal for me. This was a very dangerous time. Upon returning home, I was under strict orders to not have any visitors. If I caught even a minor cold, it could progress into pneumonia, and that would be the end of me. Everything had to be sterilized and cooked very well. The worst thing was I couldn't see any of my grandchildren, because they were walking germs.

Well, thank God, I am now in total remission. The best thing that happened before my illness was Jay and Andrea became engaged. He brought her to The Manor, one of the most beautiful restaurants in Jersey. He popped the question outside on the beautiful grounds

131

in their gazebo. It was so romantic. So when I was so sick, and wanted to give up, I would start thinking about their wedding, and how I had to make it. And make it I did! He and Andrea were married on January 25, 2014. I was so thankful to be there when he took his beautiful bride as his wife.

On a snowy winter's day, they were married at Saint Vincent Martyr Church in Madison, and had their reception at Primavera Regency in Stirling. I danced with Jay to the song I sang to him when he was a baby, "For Once in My Life;" and the main line is, "I have someone who needs me." I wanted a baby so badly, and really needed to be needed. The reception was amazing with a cocktail hour, full dinner, and a Viennese Table with every kind of dessert you can imagine. It was just wonderful!

I am so thankful for Andrea. She and Jay really helped us when I had the stem cell transplant. Andrea, Jay, and Glen came with us to hear the instructions for my return home, and Andrea and Jay completely took over. As the oldest child in the family, that's what you do. They made sure everything was sterilized, and they didn't allow anyone to come over to see me since we had to watch out for germs. It took Jay a long time to get married, but he found the perfect girl for himself. She is not only beautiful on the outside, but even more beautiful on the inside. She is not only there for me, but for everyone. She is smart and is very ambitious.

Andrea is a manager in banking. She is fantastic with children, and they just gravitate to her. Well, as you can imagine, she wants to have a baby as soon as possible. I thank God for her and all my daughters and sons-in-law. I couldn't have done better if I had picked them out myself. The best thing of all is they all get along well. They are always doing something to help each other, and they have a lot of fun together. God is so good. We couldn't ask for anything more as parents.

We have so much to look forward to this year, as my daughter Jean is having her second baby in March. It's going to be a little girl. She didn't want to wait to know the gender of the baby. She and Dom had a "baby reveal" party. Her doctor put the gender of the baby in an envelope and sealed it. Jean then took it to Party City, and without her knowing, they put the appropriate color balloons in a big box. Well, at the end of the party she opened the box, and released the balloons. When she saw they were pink, she was thrilled. Now she'd have a boy *and* a little girl. I just prayed she was healthy.

Bea and Jim

So as you can see, I was much needed. We raised six children, took care of our elderly parents, went through Jim's and my illnesses, and now we have seven grandchildren. Praise the Lord! It is wonderful to be needed! He truly answered my prayers. Do you see what happens when you pray? Prayer is so powerful. You get more blessings than you can possibly imagine—pressed down, shaken up, and overflowing! Praise be to God! Of course, Jim and I look forward to having more grandchildren as I know the rest of my children aren't finished yet.

Other events Jim and I look forward to celebrating are our fiftieth wedding anniversary and my seventieth birthday. We celebrated Jim's seventieth last October. We are thinking about going on a cruise, because we have never been. Also, next year we will be having another wedding. Glen and his girlfriend Julie were engaged on Christmas Eve. After our big seven-fish dinner, a family tradition, we were all in our family room opening funny gag gifts when Glen got on one knee and proposed. We were all in shock, and no one was aware but Jean since he wanted her to take pictures of the proposal. I was crying, and all of us were so happy. He has been seeing her for the past four years. Julie is a wonderful person, and very beautiful. She is much younger than Glen, but she is so mature for her thirty years. Julie is very smart, and she has her master's degree in social work. Glen is in title insurance and is doing fairly well. My Gabrielle is eleven years old, and Michael is eight. I can't say it enough. I am a very blessed woman!

Yes, 2014 was a year we had a lot of celebrations. After Jay and Andrea's wedding, Jean had her beautiful baby girl, Ella Rose. She was eight pounds, six ounces, and was born on March nineteenth. Then all my children gave us a fiftieth anniversary surprise party at The Brownstone, a beautiful catering hall. What a difference it was from our wedding reception! We were so surprised since they had already taken us out to dinner on our anniversary day. It was wonderful to celebrate with all our friends and family. We were so thrilled that they thought to have a special party for us, and I know Gayle had a lot of ideas for it. It was no surprise to think she was in charge.

On October eighth, Dominica and Steven had their second girl, Angelina Belle. She weighed seven pounds, eight ounces. Yes, another blessing, and soon after, Gayle delivered her handsome little boy, Patrick James, weighing eight pounds, one ounce on November first. It was definitely quite a year. I don't think anything could top it.

Now that Jim and I are getting up there in years, I think the good Lord wants us to make a change, so we are selling our big house. Not that we want to, but it is getting to be too much for us to take care of, especially since we are fanatics about cleaning and keeping up the grounds. We would like to stay in town and live in a townhouse, which will be quite a change. Actually, I don't know what Jim will do with himself, but he tells me not to worry about it. I'm sure he will do something as he can never just sit around. We are hoping to travel a little as long as we feel up to it.

On November 1, 2015, our beautiful home was sold. Yes, we moved into a condo right here in Florham Park, especially since it was voted the best town in Jersey to live. Why would I ever move away? Everything is here for us. Our church, Saint Vincent Martyr, our friends, my Bible study group, and our senior citizen's club. What makes it all the better for us is my children are only twenty minutes away, most of them in Denville.

Things were pretty hectic as we were moving, and my son Glen and his beautiful bride, Julie, were getting married on November fourteenth. The wedding was so very elegant. The move was a big change for Jim and me, but we are getting used to it. As long as we are together, that's home. For me, Jim is home.

In November 2016, at our Thanksgiving Day dinner, we all went around the table saying what we were thankful for. When it was Glen's turn, he said, "We are thankful that we can give you your tenth grandchild." Three months later, they had a gender reveal dinner with a cake with blue filling inside, and it was confirmed. It was a boy! Her due date was the end of July 2017. They bought a beautiful home in East Hanover as well and would be moving in before the baby was due. The blessings just kept coming. Is my Lord good or what?

Just when I thought I had met most of any mother's expectations, and received all of the greatest news anyone can handle in the preceding months, I was blessed with even more. Jay and Andrea had been living in their one-bedroom condo for quite a while now, and they began eagerly looking for a house toward the latter part of 2016. They had seen so many homes, a lot of foreclosures, many in poor shape or in less than desirable areas. They were getting very frustrated, to say the least; and at the same time, they were diligently trying to have a baby. They had been trying naturally for some time and couldn't get pregnant. Their age and stress were all contributing factors to the lack of success. So they opted to go to a reproductive facility to see what was available and pursued alternative options.

After countless visits and two rounds of treatment, unfortunately, they still didn't get blessed with a pregnancy. Since the holidays were upon us, they decided to take a break from house shopping and baby making, and focused on the coming New Year. Well, the New Year came and they got back to it. They spent a few months trying again, and continued house shopping in search of that perfect place to call their home, and hopefully raise a family.

One weekend, in spring of 2017, they were attending an open house at a home in Succasunna, but the house wasn't too appealing to either of them. As they were leaving the neighborhood, they stumbled upon another home that was for sale. It was a pristine little split-level house with a beautifully manicured yard. They quickly called their realtor and had him set up a showing for them. They went to see it and knew right then and there that this was the one. They put a bid in and patiently awaited the seller's response.

After a couple negotiations, on a beautiful Sunday in May they were informed that the seller accepted their final offer. They were so excited and couldn't wait to bring us and Andrea's mother to see the house. We all planned to go immediately that day. So, as Jay and Andrea were home getting ready, Jay was in the bedroom, and he heard Andrea scream from the bathroom, "Oh my God!"

Jay came running, thinking she hurt herself or maybe there was a big spider in the room or something. She opened the door in tears, and with a pregnancy test in hand exclaimed, "We're pregnant!" They both fell into each other's arms, hugged, kissed, and cried; and they just couldn't believe that this day had finally come for them. And to think it was the very same day their bid was accepted for their house purchase! Although it was very early in the pregnancy, they couldn't wait to tell us. So after we went to see their prospective new home—which was beautiful, by the way—we went out to lunch. They told the story and gave us the wonderful news. We all just hugged and cried in joyful celebration of these beautiful blessings our God had bestowed on them.

Mother's Day was a few weeks away, and Jay and Andrea decided to tell the family the great news at our family gathering. Everyone was so excited, and as a mother, well, I couldn't think of a better way to celebrate or embrace this wonderful time together. Having all my six kids and their spouses together—along with my nine grand-children and two daughters-in-law pregnant with numbers ten and eleven—was one of the best Mother's Day gifts ever!

Jay and Andrea closed on their new home in July 2017, and their baby's due date was in January 2018. It's quite remarkable that my two oldest son's wives were both pregnant and buying homes around the same time. Life is funny and very unpredictable.

Amidst all this excitement, I finally had the chance to fulfill one of my lifelong desires. Jim and I took that cruise we had been dreaming about. We left out of Bayonne and took a beautiful seven-day trip to Bermuda. It was everything we had dreamed it would be and more. The weather was beautiful, the ship was amazing, and we had such a fantastic time together. We can't wait to go on another one again someday.

Bea and Jim 2018

A short time after we got home, and still flying high from our trip, we received another amazing blessing from God. Glen and Julie were scheduled to have their baby by caesarean on July thirteenth. Well, Julie was home the weekend before and began to have contractions. They were getting more intense so they called the doctor. He advised that they come to the hospital, and she went into labor. A few short hours later, on Saturday, the eighth of July, she gave birth to our tenth beautiful grandson. They named him Christian Gerard. He weighed six pounds, ten ounces, and had a full head of dark hair. He is so handsome and such a precious bundle of joy. We are all so happy for them.

Then finally the long wait was over. All of Jay's and Andrea's hard work and efforts were about to come to fruition. On Monday, the eighth of January, Andrea was experiencing high blood pressure, and her doctor advised she come straight to the hospital. They examined her, and decided to induce her as she was only a few days from her projected due date. It was a long night, but to avoid complications they chose to perform a caesarean section. The next morning, before we could get to the hospital, we got the call. My oldest son and his wife gave birth to a beautiful, healthy, baby girl at 9:49 am on January 9, 2018. They named her Stella Rose after their grandparents, and she weighed six pounds, thirteen ounces, and was nineteen and a half inches long. We all went to the hospital, and Jay came out to greet us beaming in pride as a new father to a beautiful baby girl. We all cried, hugged, and celebrated in the miracle of life that we all were experiencing. God works in miraculous ways, and He surely was looking over them throughout their pregnancy, and right until the delivery of our eleventh grandchild, beautiful Stella Rose.

When you least expect it, God comes through, surprises you, and blesses you beyond your wildest imagination. It's as if my life's gone full circle. All my children found wonderful spouses to share their lives with. They all bought beautiful homes to raise their families in and will have children to share it with, and hopefully pass on to them what I've so eagerly tried to instill in my children. I can't tell you what a rewarding feeling that is for a parent!

Well, as you can see, my life took a lot of ups and downs, twists and turns. But with God, nothing is impossible, and I can do all things through Christ who strengthens me. And I did with His help!

It was very hard writing this book. All the pain and anguish came back, but I wanted to let others know how the good Lord worked in my life every step of the way and I don't take any credit for it. And as for getting my sight back, I feel this way: in this life, my sight may never come to be, but the face of Christ is the first I'll see when at last I enter into eternity. I have fought the good fight, I have finished the race, and I have kept the faith (2 Timothy 4:7).

The end? No. It's just the beginning . . .

The Guzzi family 2018

Bea's first guide dog Becky "1997-2009"

Bea's second guide dog Beth "2007-2018"

Acknowledgement

I 'd like to acknowledge my son Jay for his help with editing my manuscript and managing the entire publishing process, my daughter Jean for her help in editing the photos throughout the book, and Christian Faith Publishing for believing in me and publishing my story. I thank you all from the bottom of my heart!

CPSIA information can be obtained
at www.ICGtesting.com
Printed in the USA
LVHW051124080920
665300LV00003B/404

9 781643 499772